Felix Guattari once wrote that 'it is not only species that are becoming extinct but also the words, phrases and gestures of human solidarity.' Tapp's journal/memoir, an exploration of a single workers strike in the age of surveillance and the police state, helps us work against this disaster perceived by Guattari years ago. *A Serf's Journal* is a powerful and much-needed overdue call for solidarity today.
Alfie Bown, *Hong Kong Review of Books*

Working dangerous jobs in an unsafe shipyard, Terry Tapp was up against oppressive company management, a corrupt union in cahoots with the company and the everyday struggle to survive on inadequate pay. But rather than be in competition with one another, he and his co-workers learn to instead cooperate with each other and even win some battles. He tells this story of working people learning to fight back with the soul of a poet and an ability to connect individual struggles with the far larger economic forces that are making life so miserable for so many.
Pete Dolack, author of *It's Not Over: Learning From the Socialist Experiment*

Every day, millions of people grind their way through miserable work. And every day, a few of them decide the status quo cannot stand — they have to fight back. Very few of either of those stories ever get told, particularly by the heroic people who lived them. Terry Tapp does both in a tale of unbelievable miserable, dangerous work and courageous, fed-up workers up against incredibly tall odds. Anyone who has worked a terrible job should read it. Anyone who has dreamed about fighting back should study it.

Micah Uetricht, *Jacobin magazine*

This is a fascinating narrative of what it's like to work as a genuine, authentic worker producing real goods in a physical dimension. Someday this book may be viewed as long-gone nostalgia, but perhaps not! Read And Enjoy...

V. Vale, founder of *Search & Destroy* and *RE/Search*; researchpubs.com

A Serf's Journal

The Story of the United States'
Longest Wildcat Strike

A Serf's Journal

The Story of the United States'
Longest Wildcat Strike

Terry Tapp

Winchester, UK
Washington, USA

First published by Zero Books, 2017
Zero Books is an imprint of John Hunt Publishing Ltd., Laurel House, Station Approach,
Alresford, Hants, SO24 9JH, UK
office1@jhpbooks.net
www.johnhuntpublishing.com
www.zero-books.net

For distributor details and how to order please visit the 'Ordering' section on our website.

Text copyright: Terry Tapp 2016

ISBN: 978 1 78535 119 8
978 1 78535 120 4 (ebook)
Library of Congress Control Number: 2016931756

All rights reserved. Except for brief quotations in critical articles or reviews, no part of this
book may be reproduced in any manner without prior written permission from the publishers.

The rights of Terry Tapp as author have been asserted in accordance with the Copyright,
Designs and Patents Act 1988.

A CIP catalogue record for this book is available from the British Library.

Design: Stuart Davies

Printed and bound by CPI Group (UK) Ltd, Croydon, CR0 4YY, UK

We operate a distinctive and ethical publishing philosophy in all
areas of our business, from our global network of authors to
production and worldwide distribution.

CONTENTS

A Serf's Journal

I worked in a shipyard, one of the largest shipyards in the United States. I was a welder, steel fitter and pipefitter there.

The Ohio River ran along the shipyard to the south. A chain-link fence bordered the northern side and rings of barbed wire ran along the top of that fence. When we came to work in the morning, we entered the shipyard through a gate in the chain-link fence. There was a shed-like building immediately after the gate with three clocks inside. We slid a plastic card with a magnetized strip on the side of any one of the clocks and walked into the shipyard past an armed guard who sat in a white, company pickup truck smoking cigarettes and reading cowboy novels.

The company installed turnstiles on one side of the clock shed, bright metal turnstiles with thick, horizontal bars that met you at eye, chest, crotch and shin level. A union steward told me the company planned to wire the turnstiles to the clocks so the turnstiles would open only when you clocked in at the beginning of shift and when you clocked out at the end of shift. They'd stay shut the rest of the time and we workers would be trapped inside the shipyard with fencing and barbed wire on one side of us and the river on the other. Like a prison.

One day I looked at that fence, that barbed wire, those turnstiles that locked us in. I was in a prison, but it felt ordinary, typical, even natural, and I thought about why that is.

*

I'm not trying to write philosophy. I am not trying to produce another book to decorate anyone's shelves. I am trying to put on a certain perspective, to look at the world in a way that will make more sense than the ways I have been taught to see things or the ways I've been forced to see things. It's an impression I'm following with a pen, the impression that our world is a prison, that our world is The Prison. These pages are glimpses of that impression and these glimpses change as I explore different aspects and moments of what may be my – and our – captivity. There are no conclusions here, just flashes, sparks, contradictions, anger, maybe some hope.

This book was written while I hid from the foremen in the shipyard. I crouched inside a makeshift, sheet metal box by the train track that runs through the shipyard where I could have been crushed by a pickup or flatbed truck riding by, but I traded that possibility for time to think and write, time to disappear. I was invisible when I wrote this. You had to look closely to catch my eyes flashing back at you from that dark place.

As I wrote this page to you, the train clanked by and spewed a black cloud of diesel exhaust. The toxic cloud came through the metal sheets and I tried to sit very still, to keep my eyes closed, and to hold my breath to avoid gagging. Sitting there I thought of a poem in which a monkey is undergoing medical research. The monkey is strapped to a board and the skin covering its skull is pulled back. There are wires attached to its exposed brain and the monkey's eyes are taped open. The poet wrote, "I believe it's our right to fly too far into a thought."

I am that monkey with its eyes bulging dry as it confronts the world. The world is that monkey as I pull the skin back from its head and slice into it with my pen. I want to see the world honestly and report that truth to you, and to me, also.

*

I drove to work at two am. The day shift began at seven am but the superintendent foreman said we're "behind" and ordered us to come in four hours early. The city was digestible at this time, all its detail contained in beams of light in front of my van or beneath a street lamp or a spotlight on the side of a building.

It seemed each light illuminated a piece of a prison.

The porch lights shone on heavy, locked doors on the houses I passed as I left my neighborhood. As I stared down from the interstate, the lights in the parking lots of businesses revealed chain-link fences or razor wire or cameras mounted on awning. The headlights of another vehicle slowly overtook me. It was a cop who drove past me and glared into my window as he slid along the highway.

Some of the pieces of the prison were still in darkness at this time. The military helicopter from Fort Knox flew above the city at this hour, its lights disguised as faint stars, as it scanned our homes for excess heat. My official papers – my driver's license and insurance and proof of registration – were in my pocket and glove compartment. The magnetic card I needed to swipe to get through the gate at work was in my pocket, too. When I entered the gate, the camera, which was dark, would come to life for a second and hurl a tiny red light as it captured my image.

It's as though these pieces – the razor wire, chain-link fence, cop, helicopter, identification papers – were waiting to be assembled into an enormous and inescapable prison. Who's to say they aren't already assembled? What evidence is there to prove otherwise? Maybe the prison was assembled long ago and we couldn't see it because we're born into it and it felt natural. Maybe all prisons feel natural after enough time has passed.

But a prison isn't just a collection of razor wire and cameras. I could stack all of the pieces in a pile and they wouldn't make a prison. Adding a cop and a guard won't turn them into a prison either. Even adding you and me – as prisoners – leaves something out.

*

Jim was an alternate union steward at the shipyard. He rode his bike to Sturgis every year for the festival and he used to take his nephew Steve with him. They'd each get a new tattoo to commemorate the event and Jim would use up most of his two week vacation (earned by years of work) riding the backroads between South Dakota and Kentucky on a Harley-Davidson Sportster.

Three years ago, Steve parked his motorcycle by the side of the road near a thick woods of maple, oak and kudzu. He had planted a couple of dozen pot plants in those woods and he wanted to check on them and to clip them back if necessary. Steve's crop was small and his infrequent stops by the area went unnoticed, but that day a state trooper watched him walk into the woods. The state trooper got curious about the parked bike and Steve ended up being charged with a series of felonies. Since he had been convicted of growing marijuana in the past, he received a fairly long sentence for this "repeat offense." He was shipped from prison to prison over the course of seven months until he wound up in North Carolina. In prison, he worked for a major clothing manufacturer and made $.25 an hour most of which the prison took for room and board.

Jim and Steve exchanged letters for the first couple of months of Steve's sentence, but soon Steve stopped writing back. When Jim called his sister to find out what was wrong with his nephew, he learned that Steve had been killed. A dozen or so prisoners had begun fighting and Steve was in on it or maybe he knew someone in the fight or maybe he tried to help someone who was hurt or maybe he was just very unlucky. Someone or some several people stabbed Steve twenty-four times with handmade prison knives cut and carved from plastic, glass or the rarely discovered piece of metal. He was alive when the medical unit picked him up but died before they could seriously try to stop the bleeding.

Jim told me that prison officials had no idea what the fight was about. Steve was twenty-two years old.

*

A barge is a rectangular box with a space – the hull – in the middle where cargo is stored. If the barge is going to be used to haul coal or grains, the cargo hull is open. If a company is going to haul liquids or chemicals, the cargo hull is fitted with tanks and piping and valves. On the top of the barge is a two-and-a-half-feet-wide walking space called the gunnel. When you stand on the gunnel, you can look down into the cargo hull or over the side of the barge fifteen to twenty-five feet down to the concrete.

Coby worked on the gunnel fitting up and welding into place the brackets that run along the coaming, a wall of sheet steel sitting atop the gunnel, the top of the side of the barge. Every day he'd drag a heavy black welding cable along the sheet-steel flooring of the gunnel, jerking on the cable as it became stuck on the steel kevels that towboat crews use to tie the barges together. One afternoon, he might have pulled the cable too hard or too quickly or maybe his feet were unbalanced when he tugged on it. Maybe he didn't see that the cable was caught on something, if it was caught on anything. Maybe he tripped on the welding cable. Maybe he just slipped on the metal dust or grease dotting the metal. What we know for sure is that Coby slid forward fast. He hit the side of his head on one arm of the solid, cast-steel kevel. That impact turned him perpendicular to the barge and the force hurled him over the side head first. The welding cable lassoed his left ankle and Coby swung upside-down like a pendulum halfway down the side of the barge. His hardhat lay on the concrete below and Coby's brain dangled from the side of his head. The foremen ordered no one to touch Coby until the ambulance came and so his brain hardened while everyone waited. As it scraped back and forth across the steel, the brain made a sound like small stones skimming over the thick surface of a pond. That evening the company ordered overtime work for the installation of the third safety chain along the gunnel which OSHA required. There had been only two.

Coby was twenty-three years old. He had two sons, one a

toddler, the other an infant.

I did Coby's job.

Steve didn't hurt anyone when he grew his pot. He worked as a construction carpenter, a framer, so he was poor and needed money, but he couldn't just get another job to make more money. There were few jobs in that area that paid you enough to get you out of poverty or debt if that's where you start, and we all started in debt. The judge that sentenced Steve claimed he owed a "debt to society" for growing pot. Steve went to jail to pay that debt.

Coby was paying off his debts, too. Like most of us, he had credit-card bills, rent or mortgage payments, utility bills, taxes, groceries and like Steve, he died trying to pay his debts.

Neither of these men owed me anything.

*

In the shipyard, you could easily distinguish the foremen from the workers. The foremen wore white hardhats and the workers – the welders, steel fitters, riggers, pipefitters, carpenters and painters – wore red-orange hats coated with black dust. The foremen wore clean clothing while we workers wore filthy clothes and leathers covered in metal shavings and grime. When rain's pouring or it's cold outside or it's hot outside, the foremen would stay in their offices which used to be an old, single-wide trailer mounted on cinder blocks by the river bank. That first summer I worked there the company hired a crew to construct a new building for the foremen, a large, gray box of cinder blocks with metal doors and loud locks and a sign that read, "Foremen Only!"

After the crew finished the building and the foremen moved in, they held a meeting with all the workers in my area and told us we were behind in our work. There would be a lot of overtime until we caught up. The thought of working in that place all of the time made us sick, but we put up with it since we all badly needed the money. At the end of the meeting, Ed, our union steward for the area, and the alternate steward passed around a petition to name the building after Coby and to get a plaque made with his name on it even if we had to pay for it ourselves. When the petition reached the head foreman, the superintendent foreman, he laughed and told us the company would never go for it. He put the petition on a table in the back of the meeting room and it laid there for weeks until someone threw it away.

Whatever is needed to turn a cop and a guard and a pile of razor wire, chain-link fencing, cameras and locks into a prison, I have a suspicion it hides somewhere in the stories of Steve's and Coby's deaths.

*

I started my job at the shipyard in the spring of 1999. I needed a job that had insurance since my wife was pregnant but I bought the paper every day and searched through the Help Wanted ads and all I found were $6-an-hour janitorial jobs or part-time line-cook positions or maybe-you'll-work-today, low-paying construction jobs. I'd done those kinds of job and managed to get fired from or fuck up each and every one of them. I noticed sales positions and temp jobs but I didn't even consider them anymore; I'd tried both and they made me homicidal. My sales job consisted of attempting to screw people out of their money in exchange for some overpriced mausoleum crypt or burial plot. We met in a graveyard that had almost been lost to financial ruin by the local owner as he struggled against a graveyard industry monopoly led by a Canadian billionaire. He finally caved in and sold his business and property to that billionaire. I remember the flat winter sky, the mist-dripping trees and the highway growling behind the rusted chain-link fence. I got a migraine every time I drove through the gate of that fence.

A guy from Connecticut named Mr. Moldt ran the sales

training. Moldt was short and plump and only wore pastel-pink or yellow shirts and white slacks. He taught us how to lie to people about the amount and length of payments they'd be making.

"Get them on the payment plan," he laughed, "they never take time to figure out how much they're really going to be shelling out."

He gave us a book of heart-wrenching stories of dead or dying mothers, children, papaws and orphans.

"These are sure to close the sale and they're guaranteed true," he claimed and grinned.

I wore my only full suit: polyester, dark-blue. My grandfather left it to me. I chain-smoked and tried to get people to think about their death and how close it was, but lying made me sick and several weeks into the job black rings formed around my eyes. I looked like I'd been punched and that ruined my sales presentation.

I ended up calling a temp agency.

Temping is uncertain as far as the money goes. You're likely to wind up paying for a bus ride to a private dump contracted by the city where you shovel garbage while standing in piles of glass and hypodermic needles. I was lucky and got a warehouse job through the temp agency. The warehouse was on the southern outskirts of town with no bus anywhere in sight. They worked us like dogs for a total of four hours then told us we'd worked so hard we'd completed the job early and they sent us home. For that day I grossed $24.

I fantasized about butchering my bosses, getting them in a headlock and slitting their throats and bleeding them out like hogs, but that anger ate me up and I didn't want to spend time in a state prison or death row due to one of those no-accounts so I took a new approach. My last set of lousy jobs before the shipyard was at various restaurants as a cook and on those jobs we slowed the work down when we were treated too awfully or sabotaged equipment or, in one case in which the restaurant manager attempted to force the staff to work for three hours for free, we walked out of his restaurant in front of the owner. I learned something vital from these activities.

*

At ground level the world I lived in was an ugly, gray road warted with Walmarts and check-cashing centers, fast-food franchises and churches, car dealerships, strip bars and gas stations. When I thought of that road stretching out forever, I wanted to evaporate or to simply never have been born, never know there was anything else possible. Below the gray road people were painting and drawing, playing music and dancing, writing, dreaming. They're practicing another world, my world, hidden many fathoms beneath the cracking asphalt. I drove along the ugly road to get to the shipyard and I wondered who decided things had to be this way.

It wasn't me.

*

The shipyard is one of the oldest in the United States. Workers made steamboats there in the 1800s. A local family owned the shipyard back then and their Victorian-style estate – now a museum – still sits across from the shipyard. It has large windows that face the river and I imagine the family sitting in front of those windows pointing their pale, oval faces at the workers as they built their steamboats. At some point the US government acquired the shipyard but they sold it to private owners in 1938, just in time for the new owners to make a lot of money building ships for the US Navy in World War II. Most of the large equipment we used in the shipyard dated from around that time. Sometime later the railroad company, CSX, owned controlling shares in the shipyard. In the late 1990s, CSX lost their majority position to Citicorp.

There were two buildings for the administrative staff of the shipyard. The larger building was off limits to workers. I had no idea what went on in there. The second building housed the human-resources department, labor relations, safety and first aid. It also contained several large rooms that were used for training. These rooms were lined with aspirin-blue carpet and covered with photos of busy, serious men working – welding, cutting steel, rigging sheets of metal to cranes – and photos of smiling, clean-cut men in white shirts and white hardhats shaking hands with other smiling, clean-cut men in suits and white hardhats. There's a coffee machine in the corner of the room but there's no coffee and no filters. There's not really a damned thing there at all but a dirty coffee pot and a used styrofoam cup with a cigarette butt squashed in it. I was supposed to be in this room at seven o'clock am sharp to meet the trainer but at seven twenty-five a group of men like me sat and waited alone. I got up and wandered past the coffee pot where I saw a poster on the wall featuring a picture of a hand. The hand is blood-red and curled like a frozen crab. The words below it tell me that it's my respon- sibility not to do this to myself and the best way to avoid doing this to myself is to watch out for places where my hands could be cut off, but I was applying for a job in exactly that sort of place and in fact most of the jobs available were of that kind so I didn't know what to make of the sign. Maybe it was a joke.

At seven forty a.m. our instructor showed up. He slammed down a stack of binders so new I could smell the plastic across the room – plastic I was sure was manufactured by some poor assholes in China without any concern for their welfare as they breathed that poison – then he grabbed the attendance sheet.

"Two of you were late," he said, "is that going to be a problem?"

A black man in a crumpled, tan windbreaker coughed. "No,

sir."

Our instructor nodded then gave us a lecture about work ethics, on-the-job safety, being concerned about the company "as if we owned it," and how that job had good benefits and there were a lot of other guys out there ready to fill our shoes if we decided we didn't want to work. There's a scrap of paper next to me on the table and a couple of number-two pencils. I grabbed one and sketched this guy as he talked. He's blond, about five feet, nine inches tall, cream-colored hair and a cream-colored mustache, dressed in tight, new blue jeans and a cotton, candy-yellow knit shirt. He must weigh at least two-hundred and fifty pounds; his belly's avalanching over his belt and he's got droopy, triangular man-tits. His puffy cheeks pushed his face into a crack: he'd suffocate if he stood in a freezer too long. He wore mirrored glasses and I guessed he's ex-military, rent-a-cop or a soldier-wannabe, which he soon confirmed.

"Be on time tomorrow. I'm a former Navy man." He puts his thumbs in the front pockets of his jeans, "I'm here to help you but I got no tolerance for fuckups."

Safety training was required and this guy's the safety coordinator but we spent the day getting lectured about punctuality and keeping track of our hours because the computer always makes a mistake and, has anyone in here every been in the Navy? He's short-tempered with us from the beginning and he paused in the middle of each sentence just long enough that, the moment we responded, we were interrupting him, which he made a point of mentioning many times. Eventually he told us we could go home.

"Remember what we went over today," he warned us as we left, "you'll be tested on it tomorrow."

It's two thirty in the afternoon.

I stood on the steps of the one building I was permitted to enter, waiting for my ride. A tall white guy with long, dirty-blond hair and a red bandana told me that a friend of his worked here for seven years.

"You can make some good money," he said, "they work you twentyfour seven."

"Why'd your friend leave?" I asked him.

"He got a finger cut off by the train one evening or caught in a ddog and they decided he couldn't do his job after that. Insurance here screwed him over, too."

He pointed to a blue and white train engine soaked with black grease and soot slowly moving through the middle of the shipyard, dragging a line of flat cars behind it loaded with sheet metal.

"There it goes now."

For a second I thought he was referring to the severed finger and I imagined it curled up and wiggled into hiding as the train passed.

The next day our Navy man was late again and when he finally arrived he was angrier than the previous day. He spent half the day bitterly reading page after page of notes on shipyard safety, reading them so fast I caught very little of what he said. "We need to move if a crane is lowering something on top of us. Don't weld in the rain or you'll get electrocuted. Pace yourself and work slowly if you're working in extreme heat or cold or you'll get a heatstroke or a heart attack. Wear a life jacket if you're working on the repair docks." I nodded off , sketched, and nodded off again until noon.

At lunch a secretary brought an armload of pizzas and we ate "on the company's dime."

"We figured you all would be a little hungry since you aren't being paid," our instructor said and laughed. No one responded.

After lunch we were handed respirators. We ran in place and sniffed a stinky smoke in order to prove we understood how to use the respirator.

"You'll puke if you're mistaken," the instructor said.

We all passed. The day was almost over and a guy with black

dust under his fingernails came to tell us about the union. The instructor left and the black fingernail man lit a cigarette.

"What am I supposed to tell you," he said and looked up to let the smoke gently inch over his lips before taking flight. "It's a union. They want their money just like the company. Don't bother them and they won't bother you."

He gave a resigned smile. A skinny man with a tight face who sat in the front of room raised his hand. "I have a question about the insurance," he asked. "It sucks," the black fingernail man shouted and laughed. "Don't tell me you took this job just to get the fucking insurance." He took another drag on his cigarette and said we were free to go.

As I walked out the front doors of the one building I was allowed to enter, a black man with dreads turned to me, rubbed his hands together and said, "Now we can start getting paid."

*

When I started work at the shipyard, I was hired as a laborer, the position in which almost everyone begins. I swept the gunnel and collected slag and scrap metal in gray buckets. I threw the garbage in dumpsters and the metal in bins that got picked up by trucks and taken to recycling centers. Most of my day consisted of cleaning out the sideboxes and cargo hulls of barges. The sideboxes are narrow but tall tunnels that run the length and height of the barge. They're filled with metal angles welded to the walls parallel to the bottom of the barge and diagonally across the corridor. There's a ladder you climb to get to a manhole which opens onto the gunnel. On the river, a worker on the towboat hauling the barge would climb down that ladder and crawl through the sidebox. If the barge was leaking, the leak would show up in the sidebox first. I crawled through the sideholes of barges shimmying my way to the top of the box by balancing on those metal angles.

I'd been there about a month and I was sweeping along the gunnel of a barge. I was on portside which, in the orientation of the shipyard, is north and stays in the shade for most of dayshift. I crouched down in that shade and I heard a harmonica playing softly, something very bluesy and loose. I followed the sound to the stern and there I saw a guy wearing a camo t-shirt and sitting on his orange hardhat near the edge of the barge. Behind him stood a man with curly brown hair wiggling out from under his hat and a belly like a beach ball crammed under his yellow shirt. Harmonica man stopped playing and they both glared at me as I turned the corner.

"What're you playing? I asked harmonica man who told me it was something he was inventing as he played it.

"It's based on an old tune called 'Get Me the Fuck Off this Boat!'" The two of them studied me. "You ever heard it?"

"No," I said, "but I think I've been writing the lyrics in my head for a while now."

They both smiled and looked at each other. Harmonica man jumped up.

"My name's Tom and this is um," he pointed his thumb at the mustached man, "what's your name again?"

"Shitty, my name is Shitty."

"Oh yeah. This is Shitty."

Shitty's laugh leapt over the side of the barge like a runaway. It was a thick, bell-like laugh and I got the feeling he guarded it fiercely. I liked both of them instantly.

Tom invited me to have a seat on the deck of the stern where there was shade provided by the nearly five-foot-high coaming which lined the cargo hull.

"From here you can survey a lot of the shipyard," he told me.

A hundred yards or so across the railroad tracks men worked on the gunnel of a tanker and I watched them turn to look at us. Tom tapped me on the shoulder.

"They got orange hats. Anybody with an orange hat is okay.

They're union. They aren't gonna turn you in." He put the harmonica to his lips and paused. "Just watch out for the fucking white hats. They're out to kill us."

He blew a twangy, metal staircase of music that descended to the river's edge and floated above the water with the circling river gulls.

Tom wrote poetry and as days and weeks passed and the heat of the summer grew, I christened him Official Poet of the Shithole by the River's Edge.

"I accept my title with honor," he said, bowing as we hid behind a storage building after the nine o'clock break. "I'll bring some of my poems in for you," he warned me as we casually wandered back to the barge.

We'd been hiding for a half of an hour.

"We need to grab all the break time we can. You know why?" I shook my head. "You never know when they'll say we're behind and put us on ten, twelve, fourteen or even sixteen hours days until we catch up."

Tom was forty-six years old. His hair'd gone gray and his eyes were fixed wide like a dog that's been slung against a brick wall and his head's just about to slam into it. His wife worked at the General Electric plant in Bloomington, Indiana but the plant moved out of the country so Tom left his job as a fry cook at Long John Silver's and became a rigger here. When the foremen screamed at him, Tom sometimes fell to the ground and did pushups until everyone laughed. The foremen would still be yelling when he popped up from the last pushup and danced in circles around them. He had two or three distinct dances he performed, going round and around the hollering foremen with their veinlaced necks.

"What do you think that shit is about?" he asked me, smirking, then guffawed and for the first time I noticed he had no teeth.

*

In the summer heat, my head softened like an overworked radiator. All the color faded from my eyes and the whispering voices shut up and I was certainly no man but, at best, something like steam, a thoughtless vapor, no images, no words flickering across the back of my skull, a presence no more substantial than a trail of cigarette smoke. In those circumstances I welcomed the transformation but it wasn't always that easy, escaping into air. Some mornings were cooler and purple clouds washed across the sky making time ache and drag and on those days I felt images and visions, stories, as they shouldered against my skin like crows in a pillow case. Most of the time I carried a piece of paper and a pen in my pocket or a small blank-paged book in the suspension of my hardhat. With these valuable and perfect scraps, I survived many things and many places.

I hauled metal scrap along the gunnel of a barge, back and forth, back and forth, back and forth. Down in the cargo hull the sperm-whale-gray walls were spattered with rust in hues ranging from camel-hair-sepia orange to pure-hate-heart red. Trails and explosions of white calcium laced the scene together and I was amazed at and grateful for this unmistakeable valentine from the secret world.

The humidity of morning turned to mist and then to light rain while I looked out over the barge, up the Ohio River as it bent toward Louisville. Everything was variations on a gray theme; metallic and soft, fish-violet, warm-blue flatness, bottomless-pit gray. The rain came down harder until it was a downpour and I was drenched. Everyone was shaking the water off themselves and everywhere foremen were shouting and pointing, growling into crackling walkie talkies. In the cargo hull a bank of welding machines hissed like a nest of monstrous hornets and the men who had been standing by them rapidly backed up. On the gravel below me Tom bowed his head under the rain's assault. He glanced up at me for a second then shrugged his shoulders.

Across the rail tracks men ran to one of the entrances to a sidebox that lay flat on its side. A latticework of angles – the guts of the sidebox – were revealed and in those guts I could see a pair of legs being shaken like something out of the Old Testament had ahold of them. Suddenly the legs dangled limp from the edge of the black hole. The legs were fat and wrapped with a dark blue uniform. Three men began dragging the legs out of the metal frame only to find they were attached to the walrus body of a now completely quiet man. They put him on a cot and carried him to the other side of the tanker, then they were gone. From the collection of welding machines blue sparks arced through the wet air and a man who stood nearby shook his arms and threw off his welding gloves as the rain smashed into the hot metal and fizzed.

*

Our tools were kept in a large, makeshift, metal box that we referred to as a "gang box." Inside our gang box was a stick-on thermometer which showed the temperature to be ninety-five degrees. Before dawn the radio said the humidity level was ninety percent. Someone measured the heat slowly sizzling up at us from the sheet metal as one-hundred and ten degrees. I hauled metal scrap in buckets off the barge all morning and the usual voices in my head melted away. A man named Tony walked around the floor of the hull past me. He looked lost, but he always looked lost. He was forty or so, five feet three inches with thick yellow hair parted on the side and plastered down. He was a dead ringer for Barney Rubble; I could easily picture him riding a blue, polka-dotted brontosaurus. Tom told me Tony still lived with his mom and dad.

"He's still a virgin," Tom added.

I glanced back at Tom to let him know that nobody cared one way or another about Tony's romantic life, but we both started laughing.

Tony rushed up to me.

"D'you hear what happened? A guy got killed last week. Down there in sideboxes."

"No, he didn't," I told him. "I asked the union steward about it. The guy was flat-welding, he got wet, and that AC current grabbed him and beat him like a wet towel. I heard he's got some broken bones. I saw it happen, well, some of it. He's lucky he's alive."

I walked away but he followed me like a puppy.

"Hey, why do we work in the rain anyway? It's against the law."

"It's wrong and it's a violation of safety regulations, I'm pretty sure of that, but I'm still new here. You've been here for what, ten years? You tell me why you work in the rain?"

He shook his head.

"It's real dangerous. I know there's a grievance that's been filed over it, but that was some time ago. Nothin's happened on it."

"We could just walk off the job," I said, "and get the hell out of it next time."

"Yeah, well, they'll fire you if you do, and the union sure won't have your back."

Several days later I walked through the shipyard in the purple predawn. Straight ahead of me a barge lay roped to the launch cradles. Every day three workers grabbed axes and – on the count of three – chopped clean the ropes that held the cradles and the three-hundred-ton barge would go airborne, whooshing down the slope to the river and slapping a wall of water into the sky. I was picturing the gray or red barge splitting the deep green water when I noticed that the barge in front of me was completely black. Other barges near the river were black, also. As I got closer I saw the barges swarmed with a carpet of mayflies. They came out at this time of the year to breed and die, their dead bodies providing nitrogen for the soil which is a waste now since the soil has been covered with white gravel rocks and concrete. Above the barge, the air was pockmarked with mayflies and they coated my arms and face and hardhat. At lunchtime I walked down to the launchway and Tom ran up to me from the grass and mud wearing a green camo shirt and camo pants. He swatted at his head and spat.

"Nazi bugs fucking in my eyes!" he yelled and yanked off his goggles.

I could see the mayflies still attached in a ring around his eye sockets. He took a work glove, peeled off the flies, then he reached into his pocket and removed something.

"I got a book for you," he said and handed me a stack of paper. "It's some of my poetry," he said and shrugged. "Carry it with you in this place. Read it now and then. Might keep you sane."

I thanked him and we turned toward the line of barges when a foreman walked by with a handful of envelopes.

"That's our bonus checks," Tom pointed out.

I was glad to hear that as any extra money helped. The foreman asked our names, looked over the envelopes then hand one to Tom and one to me. We opened them simultaneously as the foreman walked away. My check was for $8.

"What the hell is this bullshit?!" I heard several people yell.

"Eight, goddamned bucks?" I said to Tom, stunned.

"Yeah, appreciation for hard work." Tom shook his head and put his goggles back on.

*

The heat was beginning to increase. So far that morning the temperature had been pleasant but soon we'd be broiling especially out there on the gravel and asphalt and sheet steel. One guy told me the temperature gets up to a hundred and forty inside the sideboxes and that's not taking into account the person in that box may be wearing welding leathers. Today it's just hot, not murderous, and there's a hint of rain in the air.

By midday, clouds spread across the sky and drizzle hits my face. Larry, one of the foremen, a squat, tubby man with a tight, salt-and-pepper mustache, told me to clean out the sideboxes of the number-two position barge. The barges were numbered according to their position along the line. The lower the number – all the way down to zero – the closer they were to completion. I got a respirator, a bucket, whisk broom, flashlight and a metal scoop and crawled through the hole in the wall of the cargo hull. My job was to climb twelve feet up or so to the top of the sidebox and sweep all the slag and metal dust that fell on the angles along the wall down. You climbed these boxes by using the two-inch angles as steps and pushed yourself against the walls. Eventually I'd worked down to floor level, swept up that mess and carried it all out in a bucket through the hole. It was hot outside the box but inside it already felt like a hundred degrees or more.

By afternoon I was soaked with sweat and the temperature dropped. I was at the top of a sidebox, perched on angles. My respirator was clogged and my safety glasses fogged up from the change in the weather. The restricted breathing along with the blurry vision was putting me to sleep; I worked in a trance and lost track of time.

I eased my way down the sidebox and crawled into the cargo hull through the small hole in the wall. The rain was mist now and the sky silver. A foreman grabbed my arm as I climbed the ladder out of the hull.

"Where you going?"

I told him I had to piss and I jerked my arm away. The foremen usually tried to prevent or at least discourage us from taking breaks but they don't want you to shit on your shoes so bathroom privileges remained intact. That's useful knowledge if you're exhausted and need to chill out for a minute.

Down below no one seemed to be watching so I dodged the bathrooms and slipped into the locker room for a moment of peace. There's a man sitting on a bench taking off his leather welding sleeves and leggings.

"You going home?" I asked him.

"Being sent home," he told me.

I took a seat on the opposite bench and asked him why they're making him leave and he said, "'Cause I don't want to be electrocuted. They fucking want us to weld in the rain. How stupid is that? They wouldn't be doing it if it was their asses on the line."

"So they're sending you home because you won't work in the rain?"

"No, they're firing me 'cause I refused to work in the rain. That's insubordination. We filled up the whole breakroom over there when it started pouring and then the foremen come and tell us to get out there and work. Fuck that shit. Everybody else gets scared and heads out but me. I stay put. Now I'm suspended which really means they're gonna keep me in limbo – not working, you know, no money – until my case is arbitrated. And that means until I just go away. You can't buy groceries with nothing."

"The union won't do anything?" I asked.

"They can kiss my ass," he said, then his expressions changed. "I'm Dennis. Where the hell were you?"

"Terry. I was in a sidebox. I couldn't hear a damn thing."

"You know, another reason nobody'd stick by me is 'cause I'm black and so many of them are white."

"Could be."

"Could be?" he snorted. "Anyway, they're doing me a favor. I got a little drywall business on the side. That's the only way you can make it nowadays. I'll put my time into that now and not have to deal with their shit."

I wished him good luck and headed back up to the barge.

*

For two weeks the temperature stayed around ninety-five degrees and the humidity level bettered it. On the barges it's at least a hundred degrees; after working thirty minutes I could ring out my shirt. In fact, on these very hot day, my clothes would eventually be stiff with salt from sweating and drying over and over again. My skin became soft from sweating and when I accidentally placed my arm on a seam that had just been welded, my flesh sizzled and melted away in a white circle but, for a moment or so at least, I felt nothing. Eight hours of that heat drained my energy but they ordered us to work ten hours a day.

"It's because we're behind," our union steward told me.

I had no idea what he meant since we seemed to be working the same amount each day. I felt the soft, velvet-lined interior of my skull grow hard against the backdrop of the iron summer sky.

Sam, one of the lesser-of-an-asshole foremen, asked me to weld the side of a manhole that'd broken loose. I put the gray rod into the weld stinger and knelt down on the floor of the cargo hull. The heat of the welding arc was lost in the broiling air and I faded out; when I rose, the sky had thickened and thin rain needles hit my arm and back. Ghosts of steam rose from the sheet metal and I watched them as the rain began to cool me. Then the rain came down in thumbsized bullets.

"This is how a man gets electrocuted," a guy to my right said as he threw his welding stinger and whip onto the cargo floor.

Tony scampered from behind me and hurriedly picked up the welding gear.

"You'd better not let them see you doing that," he said as he handed the man back his equipment. "They fired a guy for doing that once. It's 'destruction of company property,'" he said and turned to me.

I looked up and the rain pounded into my face and streamed down and it felt fantastic. Above and around the hull men stood on the gunnel, rake and stern gesturing angrily, some throwing things down, others yelling. The rain was beginning to hammer us.

"So what we supposed to do now?" Tony asked and tapped on my shoulder. "We just gonna walk off?"

I talked to a lot of other workers and got a bellyful of stories about near-electrocutions and painful shocks and all the dangers of being forced to weld in the rain. I knew soon it would be me welding and I wondered if I was going home hurt or going home at all, but I couldn't lose this job. We couldn't pay our bills while I worked; imagine if I were unemployed.

Without much more thought, I walked up the ladder that led into the cargo hull. I stood for a moment on the platform at top looking down at Tony and everyone else who worked down in the hull and across at those who worked on top, and I walked down the ladder. Behind me others, some already walking off the job, followed yelling "Hell, yeah!" and "Fuck this!" I walked to the breakroom and took a seat on the dirty, gray bench of a dirty, gray picnic table. Soon the breakroom overflowed with men in wet cloths. Cigarette smoke drifted over my head.

Fifteen minutes passed and the breakroom doors blasted open. Larry pointed to the rainy world outside.

"Let's go!" he shouted.

No one said anything.

"What's wrong? Y'all deaf? I said let's go! We got shit to do! Anybody in here want a pink slip?"

In the breakroom only our eyes moved. Larry spat out "Shit fire!" and disappeared out the door into the rain. Ten minutes later he was back with the same routine but we relaxed, laughed and played cards and no one stood up. I watched Larry barrel toward the door. Just as he got to it, he kicked the door and spun around on his heels.

"I think I need a union steward here," he said and his eyebrows rose, "I gotta start dismissing some of you."

He noticed me. Of all the guys in that room, I was the only one who wore a yellow hardhat; I was on probation, not yet in the union and he could fire me at will, with or without reason. He came close and stood beside me, so close I could feel the heat of his hip on my shoulder.

"Didn't you fucking hear me?"

The eyes watched me. In my head I said goodbye to that job and wondered what I was going to tell my wife.

"I heard you," I answered and looked straight ahead.

"Then let's go!" he barked and I rotated on my ass, curved my head around him to look out the windows of the breakroom doors to the outside where the rain still fell. Quietly – since everything seemed hushed at that moment – I said, "I'm going to get right back to work as soon as it stops raining." He stood beside me for a minute then finally spat, "Shit fire!" and left. After he left, the lazy talk and laughter and mock anger gently rose like a returning tide, but my head hurt.

The rain ended after another fifteen minutes or so and Larry held the door open for us as we silently rose and drifted out of the breakroom. I walked to the ladder to climb back aboard the barge and Tony tapped me on my back.

"Hey," he said and shrugged his shoulders, squinted his eyes at me. "At least you're not a total shit talker."

*

Three men approached me as I left the shipyard that day. One was a pipe welder named Paul Knight, another was Dave Mueller, an alternate steward in the shipyard, and the third was Jim McConahey, a steel fitter on the hopper line. They were in the breakroom that afternoon and saw what happened.

"This kind of shit goes on all the time," Dave said and the others shook their heads. "Everybody sees it happen but doesn't think it goes on in all the other areas of the yard, too."

"We oughta have a meeting about this, get as many folks together as possible, start coordinating ourselves a bit," I suggested.

We decided to spread the word and meet the following week in Port Jefferson Park, right by the shipyard.

"They'll find out about it and fire us or put snipers on us," McConahey added.

The meeting in the park was straightforward and no snipers appeared, if snipers can ever be said to appear. We talked about the safety violations occurring all across the shipyard, those that occurred because the company wasn't enforcing safety regulations and those that occurred because the company was actively pushing us to violate safety protocol. We talked about our low pay or lower-than-standard pay. We talked about the union which had a history of working hand-in-hand with the company. Stories were told of the union flipping coins over worker's jobs and golfing with administrators on the company payroll and on union time. Most importantly, we decided to put together a small newsletter and distribute it throughout the shipyard. This way we'd get accurate information into folks' hands about the conditions inside the shipyard.

"They'll fire us for making that newsletter, much less passing it out inside the yard," Mueller warned us. "So we're going to be smart about how we get it in and circulate it," I said and Mueller suggested we bring it in stuck inside our hardhats or welding vests, rolled and crammed in boots, folded into lunch boxes.

*

We entered late July and the air felt like it had blown out of an oven full of rattlesnake hides. Before dawn, a foreman asked me to weld components into place on the rake of the barge but when the sun came up there was so much sweat pouring from my forehead and steaming up my goggles I could barely see what I was doing. I took off my safety glasses and I saw older men stripping their shirts off and splashing water on themselves. Their bodies shook and quivered in the thick air. The only good thing about this heat was that we were left alone; you usually wouldn't find a foreman out there. We could have, or really, should have, taken a break and gotten out of that miserableness. And during the last Monday-morning safety meeting the foreman read a memo that said the company wanted us to take as many breaks as we needed – in the air-conditioned breakrooms – to avoid heatstroke, but every time any of us try to take a break there's a foreman waiting inside to run us out.

On the gravel below my friend Shaun hid behind a metal shed and waved his hand to signal me. Shaun's about six feet four, lanky with blue eyes and a shaved, very white head; I thought he was a skinhead when I first met him.

"I just hate hair, Tapp," he explained.

I first met Shaun on a Tuesday afternoon when the foremen had a meeting and so we all had a bit of time to breathe easy. He sat on a bucket flanked by guys who piddled, half-worked, talked, smoked cigarettes. To me, they were a painting; honeyed, afternoon sunlight poured across blazing scarlet hardhats, flowed over thick sepia welding leathers and ashen-gray grime, ignited the brassy metals of torches and starry-blue steel. I picked up a hemisphere of white chalk, a soapstone, and a rod used in the gouger. The chalk crumbled perfectly. It's got the feel of a pastel crayon. The soapstone was white, too, but harder; we used it to make guidelines on metal. I used the soapstone only for accents and to define a form in the light when a darker line wouldn't do. For black I broke the gouger rod which was made of graphite. With these excellent tools, I created a drawing on the side of the coaming. Three hours passed, the meeting ended and there was an eight foot by five mural that showed us at work (actually it showed us not working at all). Two days later the barge was set into the water where the mural remained for a week before the paint crew coated it with red; for nine days the black-and-white mural blazed back at the sun.

But on that hell-hot day Shaun signaled me, and with no foremen in sight, I put down my welding whip, took off my welding hood, and made my way off the barge.

"Come on, dude, let's get some relief." Shaun ducked and vanished into the darkness below the massive barge.

Huge I-beams cradled the three-hundred-ton river barge and we crawled under them and pulled up plastic buckets and scraps of cardboard for seats. A few guys had gathered oddly cut, discarded scraps of steel and welded them together into tables and chairs that we used as jagged recliners and card tables. Down there the light crackled from mercury bulbs and frantically disappearing welding rods. This was our cave, one full of apocalyptic torture furniture and low-angled light, but the steel of the barge shot the day's heat back at the sky so our subterranean hideout was relatively cool as well as private. The foremen had to nearly get on their knees to see us and they wouldn't do that.

There was a guy named Skidmore who slept upright, sitting on a bucket, leaning against a concrete pillar, beneath the number-three barge, always under the same bulkhead. Shaun introduced me to him. They played on the union softball team. Shaun claimed Skidmore had a rich father who forced Skid to get a job to "learn the value of work." Unfortunately, the story is that Skidmore's mother died soon after he began working and the young woman his father immediately married didn't get along with Skid. That meant Skidmore got none of Daddy's money, at least not until Daddy dies, if Skidmore's stepmom hasn't rewritten his will by then.

Skidmore was the little prince who traded places with a pauper boy, but somebody closed the book before he could jump back into the story and Skid's stuck playing the pauper. He responded to this situation by using large quantities of alcohol and cocaine, and by impregnating a number of different women, all of whom were well aware of their child-support rights. He's up to five kids, though some report six and I heard rumors of nine.

One Friday, after the foremen handed out our paychecks, I found Skidmore beneath a barge where he pounded his fist on a scrap-metal coffee table and spat on the ground.

"Look at this shit!" he screamed and showed me his paycheck. "This idn't legal!"

I looked. A week's pay, plus six hours of overtime and $6.70 for welding gloves – "Equipment Fee" – left him owing $6.70. Catching up on child support.

Skidmore was released from jail three years ago after serving fourteen months for not paying his child support. From then on, he spent some months nearly every year under supervised care in a psychiatric facility or a rehab center or both, and it exhausted all his Family Medical Leave and his vacation time.

Wednesday afternoon the temperature was one-hundred and four degrees and Skidmore slept in his usual position when a guy called BamBam asked him what he thought about when he was in jail.

Skidmore shook off his exhaustion and said, "I thought about my dad and how glad I was to move the fuck out of his house and get away from him and my family."

"Doesn't sound like you got far enough away," BamBam laughed.

Skidmore added, "Mostly I just thought about getting out of that fucking place."

We laughed at him and Skidmore got up and vanished into the thin crack of light that shone between the bottom of the barge and the ground level above.

Beside my left foot laid a handful of half-spent welding rods. I picked one up and made lines in the dirt. I let the rod wander and a diagram seemed to emerge, and I realized it could have easily been taken for a maze or an escape route. I continued the pattern outward but, from the moment I saw the lines as a form of getaway map, I felt the presence of barbed wire all around them. At work, all I thought about was this escape route. I kept notebooks on how to do it; grow organic vegetables, round up work as a painting contractor, rob banks, buy my own welding equipment and start my own business, scuba dive near Yellow Banks in the Ohio River and find the lost Confederate silver, grow pot. Everyone there planned the same thing. We're all plotting our big break, the day we can flip off the administrators and the president of the company and walk away from sweat and metal dust and foremen and worries over rent and mortgage and health insurance and grocery prices. For most of us, the lottery held the best chance and several guys in my area came around each Friday with a photocopy of lotto tickets and pick numbers they bought with pooled money. Some guys hoped to start their own business and escape through that, when they win. A few guys hoped that Jesus would return soon and save them from this place. Except for Jesus, all our escape routes relied on somehow getting more of the money.

I spent a lot of time beneath one barge or another during that summer and the summers that followed. It was the only way to survive the heat. The company recognized how dangerous it was to work for long in the heat; they sent out memos to the foremen, they put up safety banners, they gave us water jugs with safety slogans printed on them, they posted signs bragging about their safety record. Then they ordered the foremen to make sure we stayed on the job come-what-may and denied us access to the airconditioned breakrooms.

*

One Friday the foremen announced a yard-wide meeting at the end of shift. All six-hundred first-shift workers gathered around a stage bedecked with blue and white streamers and misspelled safety-slogan signs. Two rows of metal chairs and two industrial fans lined the stage. A dozen white men in clean white and pastel shirts and dress slacks and white hardhats casually stepped up on the stage then all sat down but one, the Safety Director, who grabbed a megaphone and began reading off a list of "massive improvements" and talked of "our vision" while in front of the stage a sea of dirty, orange hardhats bent and nodded under the sun. The vice-president of the company spoke and then so did the head of labor relations. I lost my ability to focus on what they were saying. Finally some engineer announced the winner of the "safety award" and a little man coated with grime made his way to the front of the stage and picked up his certificate for a new, cheap television set. The president of the company took the megaphone and told us to "have a safe and rewarding work experience" and announced we were free to go. A handful of workers standing by the stage limply clapped.

Beneath the barges we talked and rested. The older men favored a half-sleep state while the younger men tended toward harassment of the older men and of each other, though when the older men chose to aggravate the others they excelled. For instance, Shaun and I and four or five other men hid beneath the three-position barge when we heard our foreman screaming for Shaun.

"I better see what this is about," he said. "If Skidmore shows up, somebody remind him we got practice tonight."

He skirted away to the upper world. Immediately after Shaun left, Skidmore appeared from the other direction.

"Anybody seen Shaun?" he asked. We told him he just missed him. "Damn," Skidmore spat, "I'm missing everybody or fucking up everything lately. Sloane's trying to get me fired. I'm goddamn broke. Me and my old lady's having real problems."

An old man called Lopp, a steel fitter, took a drag on his cigarette and said, "You got one more problem. Shaun just kicked your ass off the softball team."

There was a softball team union sponsored by the union in name only: they gave no money for it and my friend Shaun was the captain of the team.

"What!? That motherfucker! I'm gonna kick his ass! He can't treat me like that. Everybody thinks they can treat me like that, but that's the fucking limit!"

"He said you can't catch flies or hit a damned ball to save your life," Lopp confessed sadly, and Skidmore lost all control. He grabbed pieces of metal and threw them against the concrete pillars. He hit the bottom of the barge with his fist. He screamed and shouted and smashed his hands against his hardhat and chest.

And, just then, Shaun returned.

"It was nothing. He wanted confirmation of a fucking overtime sheet. Just had me freaked, that fucker getting out of his office in the heat. You just know he's up to no good."

He stared at Skidmore who had momentarily stopped but was red and shaky as a skinned, vibrating finger.

"Hey dude," Shaun said and gave him the sign for peace. Skidmore threw a handful of dirt in Shaun's face, scampered around him like a monkey, his fists clenched, and spewed out cuss words then disappeared over a concrete ledge and up into the light. Shaun brushed the dirt off his face, sat down and shook his head.

"That guy's got serious problems," He looked at Lopp. "Hey old man, I told you he was about to go off big time, didn't I?" and Lopp grinned in agreement.

"That union of our's is shit," Shaun said. "They still won't put out the $135 for us to get uniforms."

All the men gathered nodded.

"They're not a real union," Lopp added. "If we had a real union, we wouldn't have to hide under the goddamned barge to get cooled off."

"And we wouldn't have to work in the fucking rain neither,"

Mueller said.

Shaun pointed a finger at Mueller. "We didn't have to work in the rain the other day."

An older guy named Mike who leaned against a pillar apparently sleeping pushed his hardhat up from his eyes. "Well," he said, "I wouldn't get used to that if I were you." He looked around the group. "You got a whole shipyard full of suckasses. I can remember back twenty years ago we wouldn'ta put up with that shit."

"We don't have to put up with it now," I said and Mike leaned back, drew his hardhat over his eyes.

"Bunch of suckasses," he said.

"They're gonna get somebody killed," Mueller said.

Since meeting Mueller in the park that summer at our first, impromptu gathering, I'd learned he was a Vietnam veteran and owned about fifty head of cattle at his farm in rural Indiana. He built his own home which impressed me until Shaun warned, "You have to see it, Tapp." Mueller had long, dirty hair which he rolled into a bun and pushed under his hardhat. Overall he was in good shape except for a beer belly that, I judged from the pile of Budweiser cans that fell out of his truck, appeared to be an ongoing project.

"If you die, these motherfuckers'll just roll you over and put somebody else in your place," Lopp laughed.

"It isn't funny," Mike mumbled and pushed his hardhat up again. "I got shocked so bad one day it threw me off the ground and back in the air about five or six feet. Knocked the shit outta me. Hell, a couple more feet and I'd've gone flying off the barge and broken my motherfucking spine."

Mueller leaned into the center of the group. "That's why we gotta stick together," he said. "Every time they order you to work in unsafe conditions ("Which they do every fucking day!" somebody behind me yelled) – well then – you gotta file a grievance. Pile enough of those grievances up and the union's gotta take notice."

A guy in a camo jacket with a red toothpick in his mouth moved to the seat beside Mueller.

"Now that's some bullshit," he said. "We been filing griev-ances for years and it ain't done any good. In fact" – he turned to the rest of us, his head cocked – "that fucking union doesn't give a shit about you. You know they flipped a damn quarter over a man's job? I know who seen it. She was a union steward over on Line Four. She told everybody about it and then she got fired, too." He looked at Mueller. "What good's any of this bullshit with grievances and the union gonna do?"

Mueller closed his eyes and raised his hands.

"I know about all of this, Paul," he said. "We got an election coming up this December. We got an independent slate running on that election. What we gotta do is get out there and vote and get rid of these damn crooks that run the local." Mueller looked around the group and said, "UPS guys don't have to do this shit; they don't have to risk their lives. They hold their own meetings. They got a newsletter comes around and tells 'em all what's going on."

Lopp chuckled. "A newsletter? Hell, half these guys can't even read."

*

One afternoon I was spot-welding for a guy on top of the barge and I saw what looked like a police car but may have been private security drive up to the dirt strip where we kept the large metal boxes we'd welded together as makeshift storage units. Two uniformed men got out of the car. They motioned to someone inside who emerged from the back seat and I saw that it was Dennis. Lopp, the guy I was working with, was crouching down measuring a steel plate. He raised up and tapped my leg with his gloved hand.

"Don't stare," he warned, "you get in trouble."

"That's Dennis," I told him. "The guy they fucked with because he wouldn't work in the rain." Lopp looked at him quickly then turned to me.

"I know who that is. He's been on suspension for five weeks. I also know he's got two security guards with him so that means they're escorting him out. Act like you got a problem with it and they'll fire you, too."

I looked around me and I couldn't see a foreman anywhere. I saw guys on top of several other barges shyly glancing down at Dennis.

My stomach tightened. I took off my equipment and walked off the barge. It wasn't a matter of bravery but of being incapable of not acting, of being so full of hatred at the situation and possibly at myself that one more drop of restraint was intolerable. The two guards stared at me with tin faces. Dennis bent down and pulled items out of his storage box. When I approached he looked up at me and smiled weakly.

"Hey man, you know you're not supposed to be here."

I asked him what's going on and he told me that he was working at his drywall business and barely paying his bills.

"But I was having trouble making ends meet when I worked here, too. At least my stress level is way down." He almost laughed and I realized he looked relaxed, given the circumstances. "Dude, you want a box?" and before I answered he stood up. "You want to some tools, too? Fuckin' have 'em." He waved his hand toward the things he had hurriedly collected, then dismissed them as he opened the back door of the guards' car, snarled at them – "Get me the fuck out of here" – and gave me a thumbs up. "Hey, thanks, man."

I wasn't sure what he was thanking me for but I took out a soapstone and wrote my name on the box before I closed it up. Later that day I bought a lock for it from the supply room.

*

On a Friday morning the temperature plummeted. The sky turned purple and let loose cool air in a sharp burst like sexual release. My mood changed from a default of blank rage to something almost two octaves lighter. At nine o'clock we got a ten-minute break and Shaun approached me as I sat down on a bench to drink coffee.

"What we doing, dude?"

"What do you mean?" I asked him.

"It's about to rain? We gonna suck ass or what?"

I studied his eyes.

"Fuck it," I said, "I'll be right here if it rains."

"Well, let's go talk to some guys on the other barges then," he suggested.

I put down my coffee and we ran across the gravel and concrete to another breakroom a hundred and fifty yards away. Inside several women and forty or so men sat on benches drinking cokes and coffees and eating vending-machine death food. Shaun lightly slapped the back of a short, plump, blondhaired woman.

"What we doing?"

"Sloane said he's got a handful of pink slips if we decide we don't want to work," she said.

"Sloane's the foreman on this barge," Shaun told me. "They used to call him the 'Terminator' 'cause he got so many people fired."

"Hey!" I yelled out to the room. "We're going to be walking back to these breakrooms when it starts raining, just so you'll know."

We raced down to another break shack and then one more before we sprinted back to number-three-position barge and returned to work.

The air filled with mist and sometimes a light sprinkle of rain appeared during the several hours that stood between us and lunch, but as soon as we climbed the ladder to the barge after lunch break, a storm overtook the sky and split it open.

"It's a fucking downpour, Tapp," Shaun groaned as the rain roared around us.

"Let's go," I said and he laughed but before we had time to move a bolt of lightning cut through the blackened sky and made my scalp tingle. "Holy shit!" I hollered and Shaun and I bolted to the ladder.

More lightning tore over us and the rain drenched our clothes. When we got to the gravel we ran past the barge behind us and a foreman approached.

"That's Sloane," Samuel yelled through the rain and I looked at the chubby man with a straw mustache, his skin blotchy like a spit-stained wall, the white hard-hat crunched onto his head sending his stringy hair shooting outward in a down-pointed halo. He planted himself at the bottom of the ladder just as the first of the workers were coming down.

"Get the fuck back up there!" he shouted and everyone stopped.

The first two in line were the short, blond-haired woman and Lopp.

"It's lightning!" Lopp barked back at him and Sloane extended his arm across the end of the ladder and blocked them from leaving.

"When you agreed to work here, you agreed to work in the elements," he said, "and you should know that this barge is grounded. You are in no danger."

"Bullshit!" the blond-haired lady yelled through the rain then ducked under Sloane's arm and ran to the breakroom.

"Alright, you son-of-a-bitch," Lopp snapped and extended his arm to grab the front of Sloane's shirt and wad it into a ball. "If it's so safe, then you get up here and supervise my ass."

Sloane yanked on Lopp's arm and stammered, "There's…

there's lightning!" Lopp released him as everyone ran to the breakroom and Lopp turned to shout "Pussy!" at Sloane whose form disappeared in the bluegray torrent.

In the breakroom I noticed Lopp was missing the ends of his right index and middle fingers. I asked him what happened.

"Got 'em cut off by a pendulum saw at the wood mill when I was eighteen," he wiggled his fingers in the the air. "They're stubs, but they're tough as nails." He rammed his two fingers onto the tabletop and guffawed as the table quaked. "I jabbed Sloane with them in the chest when I grabbed him out there."

"I wish you had killed him," I said. "I don't want to die for this fucking job and somebody's going to get killed. I felt that lightning snake down my neck."

He sipped his coffee.

"They don't care. You can bet they're gonna make us pay dearly for gettin' out of it today."

I knew he was right.

*

At the next Monday-morning safety meeting, the four foremen for our section stood in front of the breakroom like they usually did but another fellow joined them. This guy looked like a cabbage-patch doll; a jellied white man with his eyes and his mouth punched deep into him and his nose hooked like a beak, veined – when I saw him up close – like an oak leaf with blue lines.

Shaun leaned over to me and whispered, "That's Blackman. He's the superintendent foreman. There are only a couple of them over the whole shipyard."

He squinted at the front of the room.

"Everybody thinks he's Klan, too."

"Bullshit."

"It's true," Paul whispered from my other side. "And he's

dangerous. He shot his son."

"How?"

"They were hunting."

"Oh," I said, and waved him off, "accidents happen."

"He shot him twice."

"Alright, let's get this meeting going," Blackman loudly announced and the large, restless room grew still. "We been having a lot of trouble this summer with you men coming off the job."

He paused and scanned the room.

"It's got to stop. We got orders to fill and I can tell you all we're damn near getting behind again. You boys don't want to have to go on the schedule we had last fall, do you? From what I hear, some of you all's marriages didn't make it through that."

I saw several men nodding their heads in agreement. I leaned over and asked Paul what was up with that schedule.

"Twelve to fourteen hours a day, seven days a week for months," he whispered.

"Isn't that illegal?" I asked him.

"Nah," he said, "they can't work you for thirty-six days straight or something, so they give you day thirty-seven off or whatever. Then they start right back up."

Blackman chuckled and put his hands in his pockets.

"So here's what's going to happen. We talked to your union and they suggested we issue you rain jackets so here they are." He pointed to a box at his right then held up a slip of paper. "Now this here is your acknowledgment that you have received your rain equipment. Your foremen are passing these out. Make sure you sign one before you get out that door."

A middle-aged black man with a steel-wool mustache stood up and shouted, "No fuckin' raincoat's gonna keep anybody from being electrocuted! Isn't gonna keep anybody from getting sick either and missing days."

Blackman glared at the man and tightened his lips as other

men yelled.

"I ain't gonna sign this," Paul said as a foreman handed him the release form for the rain jacket.

"Yeah fuck it!" Shaun shouted and we threw our forms on the floor as everyone walked out the breakroom door.

Shaun and I headed toward the ladder as Mueller caught up with us.

"I heard tell we had everyone in this area walking off Friday," he gushed. "It was a lot of folks. We gotta try and get more."

"We could try this," I said, "instead of just walking off, we stand there for a minute and let other guys see us. That way they'll know what's going on and they won't be stranded clueless in the rain."

"We could flash 'em secret signals," Shaun grinned and wiggled his fingers in front of Mueller's face.

Mueller ignored him. "Make sure and file your grievance," he advised as we climbed the ladder.

*

We had another meeting in the park and made a more formal list of items we wanted to discuss. Several new folks attended the meeting as word had begun to spread.

"We should have the next meeting at my place down the street," one fellow said, "it's too easy to spy on us and fire us the next day."

Safety was at the top of our list along with our chintzy bonuses as well as an introduction to exactly who we were ultimately working for which, in our case, was CitiGroup, the same company that owned and controlled the banks many of us used. We decided to mention something about the upcoming union election and what a union is there for in the first place since, given the actions of our official union, it was difficult to discern this. I took our notes home with me and typed up the newsletter. The next morning we met in the parking lot before we entered the shipyard and took a number of copies each, smuggling them in in our lunchboxes or boots or hardhats. The newsletter appeared everywhere; in bathrooms and breakrooms and locker rooms and folded in gang boxes and underneath the barges. It was a hit.

The next day the rain started at about ten thirty in the morning. Shaun and I stood at the top of the ladder to the barge and two guys working atop the neighboring barge noticed us and pointed. We turned around and someone gestured from the barge behind us. We faced portside and saw Skidmore on the barge parallel to us. He gave us the thumbs up and walked off the barge as others followed. Men descended from the barges in streams down ladders and into breakrooms, into locker rooms. We had a total walk-off of our area. We waited out the rain and once it ended, once we could work safely, we emerged from doors and cracks in the earth like foxes.

*

As the summer ended, walk-offs became our favorite pastime and we perfected this wonderful art. Anytime there was rain or a storm, we simply dropped what we were doing and everyone in our area headed for a locker room or breakroom. I even saw a few folks from other areas walking off with us and heard stories about workers in other areas walking out together for specific safety violations.

This habit of standing up for one another spilled into other situations as well, not simply when the possibility of being electrocuted literally hung over us. One Wednesday in that often gorgeous place between summer and autumn in Kentucky, a guy named Crowley worked near me on the gunnel welding coaming into place. Sloane, the foreman, barreled toward him and grabbed his arm.

"You're outta here!" he yelled and tugged on Crowley's sleeve.

"What the hell are you talking about?!" Crowley asked him and Sloane explained that Crowley had been late that morning – again – and that constituted another absence, one absence over what the company and union contract agreed on as acceptable, and that meant Crowley was out of a job.

"I got a slip at home that shows I had a doctor's excuse for the last time I was late!" he exclaimed.

"Tough shit," Sloane told him, "you're out of the yard and in suspension 'til it gets resolved. Could take a few months for that to get resolved."

As this argument went on, a number of us gathered around them from both ends of the gunnel. Crowley tried again to explain to Sloane that he had the paperwork and that the house he rented was just a couple of minutes' drive from the shipyard, that he could easily go and get the paperwork, and that, if he were suspended for several months, his family would be screwed. He had two small children and his wife and he both worked long hours and a couple of jobs to support the household. Sloane told him outright he didn't give a shit.

But we did, and with a loud thunk, a couple of us dropped our tools.

"Let him get the paperwork," I said to Sloane. "It'll take ten minutes."

I looked around and saw that Shaun had dropped his tools too, the two ratchets he carried and the box of welding rods.

"Goddamn it!" Sloane shouted, "I got a certain number of man hours allotted to me for this job and if you guys don't keep working I'll go over 'em!"

"Give him ten minutes and we'll make it up," Shaun said.

"Give him nothing, fuck him over, and we'll go as slow as the dead," I added.

Crowley took off and we mingled along the gunnel, talked, exchanged stories, discussed news. Ten minutes later Crowley returned with his paperwork and we resumed our toil.

One morning I watched a clean, white pickup truck pull up next to the trailer where the foremen had their offices. Two men got out of the truck; both of them fat, white men but one was double the size of the other and, with his hardhat on, he resembled a tool shed with a cherry on top. I couldn't see his feet. He wore a pair of overalls with enough fabric to cover a Volkswagen bug. Another truck pulled up and Blackman got out. He shook the hands of both men then put his arm around – as best he could – the shoulders of the titanic man and the three disappeared into the trailer. I waited for the trailer to collapse.

"That's Tiny," Lopp said. "He's the chief steward. He's the biggest suckass you'll ever meet. That other guy's the business agent for the union."

"I wonder what they're meeting about."

"Probably planning some new way to fuck us over," Lopp said.

That afternoon as Shaun and I walked toward the gate to leave for home, Mueller came running up to us with something in his hand.

"We did it!" he exclaimed. "Take a look at this!"

He handed a piece of paper to Shaun.

"What the hell is it?"

"They're going to read it at the next safety meeting," Mueller blurted out. "It says we don't have to work when there's lightning overhead. We finally won our grievances over this."

I looked at Shaun and he bit his lip and nodded. Mueller threw his arms around both our shoulders as we walked out and sighed, "The union finally listened."

Shaun passed me the paper and I saw that it was an announcement to be posted on the bulletin boards by the gates. It stated that a specific grievance involving four men on Line Four had been acted upon. The resolution of the grievance was that if we are working and we see lightning, we're supposed to count the seconds that pass from the moment we see the lightening until we first hear thunder. There was a chart that showed us how to calculate the distance of the lightening based on the time that passed between the lightning and the thunder. When we saw lightening, we could do this calculation and that would determine if the lightening was a mile away or closer. If the lightening was closer according to our calculations, we could come off the job.

*

That next week the company published a newsletter of its own to combat the popularity of our newsletter. Unlike our newsletter, it had much higher production values, came to us semi-glossy, with blue ink on white paper, and was doubled-sided. The main section featured the president of the company and a discussion of his importance and why he was such a good person. This amounted to a listing of his corporate positions and several mentions of the fact that he was, indeed, a really good guy. One of us was featured, too, on the back of the newsletter, in a box that told of how hard this man had worked, how he'd missed no days in some awfully long amount of time, how no one had ever complained about him or his work, but we knew this guy was a suckass and we dismissed his last page honorable. What remained of the company's newsletter was boilerplate from the employee manual. The stack of company newsletters lay mostly undisturbed in the breakroom until someone tossed it into the trash a few days later.

*

This job paid well for most of the jobs in the area at that time which meant that it paid enough to cover our bills but only if you juggled them properly and didn't pay them all at once or on time.

At home we were in constant danger of having our electricity or water or gas shut off. My wife was pregnant and the baby would be born in a month or so, in the middle of November. The house was old and drafty and if they turned our heat off at that time, we would be in real trouble.

I had Sunday off and I drank a cup of coffee downstairs and read the newspaper in the room where I'd placed a drawing table and some books. Even with the heat on the room was cold as hell and some sort of black mold crawled along the northwestern wall. At least the landlord left us alone.

The local paper, the *Courier-journal*, contained a brief mention of the death of two men at the Tyson plant in Robards, Kentucky. One of the men was working near a vat of chicken parts when he fell and landed in the steaming mess. He attempted to get out but the gas from those rotting chicken guts overwhelmed him and he passed out. Other workers gathered around and planned to rescue him but there were no lifts, no harnesses, no safety chains, no standard equipment, in fact, nothing whatsoever. Some of the workers tied ropes around a chair and lowered another man down to him but that guy was overcome by the gases as well. Both men suffocated and died in that pot of gore. The first man was in his twenties with two small children, the second was in his forties. The most tragic element in this sad story is that, when a representative from the Labor Cabinet for the state of Kentucky was asked why there was no safety equipment at all, he answered that OSHA was understaffed and can only get around to inspecting a plant every three years. The Tyson plant had been open two years and I took that to mean that the plant had only been inspected upon opening or had never been inspected at all. Given that it had been open two years and no old or worn safety equipment was lying around, I took the latter interpretation.

Monday morning I was in the locker room at the shipyard and I was talking about the Tyson murders with a guy named Larry who said he knew one of the men killed.

"You're misinformed," he said, "Tyson does have some safety equipment on site. They have earplugs and safety glasses, I know that to be true, you just have to pay for them."

*

That autumn the harassment at the shipyard died down. The foremen screamed at us constantly, pushed us to work faster and faster, and someone was always having a breakdown, but nothing life-threatening occurred. We fought back and it appeared to pay off. After all, none of us wanted to be there. It was just a job that paid the bills (or, like most, didn't quite pay them) and we just didn't want to get maimed, poisoned or killed for working it. For a few weeks the morning air coming off the river carried the same vibration as the smell of very cold ice-cream, the clouds piled up and remained almost motionless in wide-eyed cobalt sky. When rain finally came, we walked out of it with little harassment.

Sloane brought our paychecks around one Friday and with them was our bonus check for that quarter. I opened the envelope containing my check before Sloane could walk away.

"A fucking $9.86 bonus?!" I yelled.

Shaun opened his as well. "Look at that, dude, $8.41. That's some bullshit."

Others shouted the amounts of their checks and several bolted toward Sloane who tried to make a getaway into the foremen's office building, but failed and found himself surrounded. I joined them.

"Gentlemen," he pleaded, his hands raised, "I do not control the amount of money you get for your bonus."

An older man with a thick red beard and mustache pushed himself at Sloane to the point that their noses were touching.

"We work like fucking dogs! You tell me how we work that goddamned hard and this is all we get for a bonus?!"

Sloane backed up and the men behind him gave him a bit of room.

"Your bonus is calculated on the number of hours you work," he explained.

I looked around me at the faces of the others as the realization hit us: the harder we worked the more work we completed, the more work we completed the more orders we filled, the more orders we filled the more money the company made, and the fewer hours it took us to fill the orders the smaller our bonus check would be. Our faces hardened and with one mind we seemed to agree that dismembering Sloane on the spot wouldn't change this overarching structure of the whole damned world.

*

One afternoon the first shift was almost over. I put my tools away and took off my work gear, leathers and so forth, and sat in the breakroom with a small sketchbook. As I drew, I thought about getting a small cup of dollar coffee from the machine. The awful, metallic-tasting coffee seemed appropriate for a tired afternoon among the smells of grinding metal and weld dust. Unfortunately the coffee machine in our breakroom was broken so I visited a nearby area and grabbed a cup there. When I returned, a large fellow with a heavy, rectangular head had my sketchbook in his hand and paged through it. I ran to him, shoved him away from my things – he dropped the sketchbook – and asked him what the hell he was doing. He struggled to say something.

"I'll kick your ass if you ever touch my things again," I warned him and, after staring at me for a few seconds, he backed up to the wall.

"I'm going to tell the government what you're writing in there."

I glared at him for a moment, then began to laugh. Over the

next couple of weeks, we became friends and I decided I wanted to paint this man, whose name was Rupe.

Rupe lived in a dilapidated apartment that smelled like shit due to an open sewer pipe running along its southern side. He sat in the one chair in his one room and I sat on the garbage-picked couch. We discussed what makes a good painting and he agreed to take off his shirt but not to be nude and I thought that was fine. I drew him sitting in his one chair with a floral-patterned cloth draped over it. He faced me straight on since, as he told me, he didn't want me to draw his side. There was a hole in his left side where a country doctor had drained water from his lungs long ago after Rupe's father or uncle had sprayed him with a hose in winter and made him sleep in the barn as punishment for backtalk. This hole embarrassed him.

When I finished drawing Rupe, he returned art for art and pulled out a stack of papers full of poems he had written. I sat back as he read a selection of them to me. The poems were completely awful, full of sing-songy rhymes and maudlin lines. The words mainly circled the shits who raised him and his long, dead mother who he missed. By the time he finished I was overcome with emotion.

The drawings I made were rich with possibility for paintings and I thanked him for posing and for sharing those poems. He thanked me for visiting and gave me a $20 bill to help with the cost of printing the newsletter.

"This is gonna get us in trouble," he admitted and shook his head, but asked me to keep doing it anyway.

*

After two days of rain, I stood atop the gunnel of the number-three-position barge looking at the scarlet light that emerged over the river when I saw a heron standing still at the river's edge. As I watched, it opened its wings and rose into the air and the white of its wings carried the green and deep blue of the water into the morning sky. The heron disappeared and I heard the sound of someone howling in pain and rage. A hundred yards off two policemen dragged a man out of a breakroom. He tossed his arms around in a circle as the cops hit him with batons, beating him around the head and shoulders. The more they beat him, the more he thrashed. A blond-haired woman came walking down the gunnel and I asked her what the hell was up.

"Happens every couple of weeks, at least," she answered, "you haven't noticed?"

I hadn't. I'd been working in the interior of the barges. The police handcuffed the man, shoved him into the back of the car which had been allowed to drive into the shipyard, and drove away.

The blond-haired woman introduced herself as Kim. She used to work as a bank teller until her husband left her.

"I can't live on a bank teller's pay," she said, "Really can't live on this pay, either, but it's a bit better."

She took care of her nine-year-old son without much help from her exhusband.

"He's a shit," she said. "Can't find a decent job. Pulling money out of him is like pulling wisdom teeth."

She talked to me about the upcoming union election. There were two other slates running beside the incumbents and she wanted me to vote for one of them.

"See, you got the mobsters, the guys that are in there now. They're no good. Then you got that Rank-and-File slate outta Detroit. Mueller's people."

She made a face.

"You gotta second group of people, independents that work for the guys in there now. They got experience and they're sick of seeing us get screwed over. I'm pushing for those folks."

"You want me to vote for a bunch of folks already working at the local, for the mobsters?"

"Yeah, but they're rebelling against the crooks," she said, "the crooks that have been running things up 'til now."

I talked with Mueller about the election and the second slate, the independents who already worked at the union hall.

"Just more mobsters. They're trying to fuck us up by dividing the vote. It's hard for me to discuss this objectively seeing as I'm on the ticket as the Rank-and-File slate's business agent for our division."

I called the Rank-and-File group's headquarters in Detroit that afternoon. The man who answered told me that he and others from Detroit had visited the shipyard two weeks ago.

"I never heard a thing about anyone visiting!" I exclaimed. "I would have liked to have met you guys."

He moaned. "I didn't think our trip down there was worth it. Really disappointed me. It's not easy to have a discussion about serious labor issues with a bunch of dirty guys with no sense of solidarity. I also got the feeling that the guys we met with were trying to make fun of us."

I asked him about this other slate, the independent-but-working-there-already slate. He claimed to know nothing about that and then told me, "Look, Mueller's a clown. It's very difficult to get him to shut up and listen. A couple of us came to the conclusion that he's at least partially retarded."

He asked me if I wanted to send him money to join his group but I told him I was broke.

Several days later the foremen began passing out two notices. The first said that union officials would be here that afternoon at the end of shift to talk to us about the upcoming election. The other said that the independent slate would be there the following day.

I saw no union officials that afternoon until I was in the line headed out at gate five, and there, immediately after the turnstile, stood two men who handed out trifolds. As I got closer I saw that one was a very tall, old man dressed in a baby-blue sports coat.

His skin was extremely light and his white hair was cut military-style, a buzz cut, and he appeared to be sleeping standing up. Beside him was a short man wearing a glossy union jacket and looking like a Southern Baptist deacon with dark sunglasses and a comb-over that consisted of no more than handful of black hairs. As I walked in front of him the old man extended his hand with the trifold and didn't look up.

I leaned forward and said, "You're a goddamned criminal," and the Baptist deacon angrily pointed for me to move on.

Across the street five men in shiny union jackets and dark sunglasses stood in a row, shoulder to shoulder, each clasping his hands in front of himself.

The next afternoon, I exited through another gate – gate eight, one of the two big gates – to avoid having to deal with the independent slate. I walked out and saw five or six gleaming, unscratched new cars, pickup trucks and SUVs parked together in our parking lot. Larry caught up to me and pointed to the collection of new vehicles.

"Damn," he said with a long emphasis on the D, "look at that, will you?"

A man who wore a shiny union jacket and dark sunglasses approached me holding a fried chicken leg in a napkin in his left hand.

"Here you go!"

I waved him away, he stuck out his right hand, and I pulled back. He smiled regardless.

"We'd appreciate your vote."

I didn't reply and I looked around to see men like him all over the parking lot. They approached workers getting off shift and all of them carried a piece of fried chicken. Colonel Sanders tried to shake my hand again.

"We can make this a better place to work if we work together."

He let his hand hang in space to make it obvious he was making an offer to me. When I didn't reciprocate he looked toward Larry.

"We're trying to lead a rebellion here, a rebellion against business-as-usual."

I walked to my van and, out of the corner of my eye, I saw Larry taking the piece of chicken. Before I turned the key in the ignition I heard him ask if they had tshirts.

The next day was Friday and that afternoon, as I left the shipyard, I saw Mueller standing by my van. He waved his hands. Several men stood beside him and the oldest, who had the contented face of a friendly grandfather, extended his hand and I took it.

"My name's Fred Stevens and I'm running on the RankandFile slate. I'd appreciate your vote."

Mueller shoved in between us.

"This is Tapp," he said, "he's one of the troublemakers."

Another guy, a younger guy named Thornsberry, took my hand.

"I work at UPS," he said, "we heard about what you guys are doing. Congratulations."

These men told me how they took their vacation time and unpaid medical leave to travel around and campaign, and how they had been harassed at each job site.

"We've had the cops called on us more than a few times," a guy with the Freight Haulers said. "It's kinda been hell a bit, but I think it's worth it."

The other men nodded their heads.

"At a couple of places, the chief steward and the company president both chased us off," the UPS guy told me. "

"A couple of places?" Fred asked, surprised. "At most places."

I took some of their literature and an armload of stickers and leaflets.

"You got my vote." We shook hands. "You got any fried chicken?"

They looked at me without understanding.

*

The next week black t-shirts that featured slogans in support of the independent slate appeared in the shipyard. On the gunnel one morning, Kim put one of the tshirts in my hand.

"I'm voting for the Rank-and-File slate," I told her. "The fried-chicken and tshirt guys are crooks."

She laughed, annoyed.

"Everyone's a crook, honey, but we gotta have somebody in charge and at least they've got experience."

"Yeah, experience fucking us over."

I gave her the shirt back.

Larry stood behind me and waited to walk around Kim and me in order to get nearer to the rake of the barge where he planned to weld up a bulkhead.

"I'll tell you who to trust, Tapp,"

He pulled a piece of paper from the right pocket of his work overalls.

"1-800-346-8290. I got that from the independent slate rep I talked to last week. He said he understands we've been working in unsafe conditions and the independent slate's gonna do something about it."

He read the number again.

"Memorize that. He said we can call them directly for assistance anytime."

I stuck some Rank-and-File stickers on the walls of the bathroom and locker room.

*

The next morning I was on top of a barge and looked down to see Mueller who stood outside of one of the shacks where we stored welding rods. A handful of men gathered around him in a loose circle. One of the men wore a camo jacket and mirrored sunglasses and he held his fists up like he was preparing to punch Mueller. As I watched, the man wove and bobbed, punched the air beside Mueller's head. When Mueller didn't react, the man slapped Mueller's hardhat off his head and the grimy, orange hat flew against the side of the welding shack. I walked to the ladder and off the barge and as I did I noticed that one of the men who circled Mueller was a foreman. By the time I reached Mueller, the men had wandered off. I asked Mueller if he's ok.

"Yeah, sure. They're trying to get me to hit them so I'll get fired. It's nothing."

*

The winter settled in and our heating bills soared past the payable level, even with expert juggling. I called the utility company and tried to work out an agreement with them, some sort of schedule. The old farmhouse I rented had two small, simple, utilitarian fireplaces, and I chopped a lot of wood to offset the need for utility heat and avoid adding more debt. My son was born at home and I didn't go into work that day but stayed by my wife at his birth. That was the day before the Thanksgiving holiday, one of two paid holidays. If you missed any work the day before or after a paid holiday, you forfeited the holiday pay. A medical emergency was the only exception.

When I returned to work on Monday, I was told I wouldn't receive my holiday pay due to my missing work the day before the holiday. Immediately after shift, I walked into the office of the guy in charge of labor relations and asked him about this. I told him my wife was giving birth that day and I stayed with her.

"Yes, ok, I understand that," he said, not looking up, "but you lost all that pay. You can read the wording yourself in your contract book."

I sat down in the chair in front of his desk. He raised his head and looked at me with what appeared to be open disgust. My clothes were covered with grease and dirt and his chair was very expensivelooking.

"The only exception is a medical emergency," he said.

He opened his mouth to ask me to get out of his chair – and out of his office – and I interrupted.

"A human head coming out of someone's pussy is a medical emergency."

He glared at me for a good ten seconds, then took a form out of his desk drawer and signed it. I got my holiday pay.

*

I wore thermal underwear to work along with a sockcap as well as knit gloves under my leather work gloves and the winter was bearable as long as the wind didn't blow. When the wind blew, you had no choice but to freeze. The first week of December was rainy and the temperature dropped far below freezing. The gates were coated with ice when we entered and they creaked only halfway until three of us shoved them fully open with a snap. In front of me a man fell on the ice-covered asphalt. I headed for the gravel but puddles of ice laid there, too. Even the handle to the breakroom door was frozen shut and we stood outside while a couple of guys went to the bathroom with a bucket to get hot water to melt it. Ice coated everything, every surface of every barge. Ice hung from the coaming. Ice dangled off the gunnel and over the side and from the three safety chains linking the frozen safety poles along the top.

I sat at a table with Shaun in the breakroom and took out a pencil and some folded paper and began to draw. Shaun tapped me on the shoulder.

"Look at that gunnel," he said, "it's fucking slick, dude. Might as well work in skates today."

"I heard they're going to send us home," a guy who sat next

to me said.

"It's not safe," Shaun added and the man shrugged.

"They don't care. Problem is, when it's this cold, the welds' will crystalize."

The foremen entered the breakroom and ordered us to get to work. As I left, Larry handed me a bag of salt and told me to spread it all along the gunnel and down in the flooring of the hull. It's a five-pound bag.

"Five pounds are gonna take care of all that surface?"

"Good enough, and one bag per barge is all we got, so we gonna make it work."

The ladder to the barge was solid ice and, as I climbed it, a man in front of me slipped and busted his shin. He cussed through clenched teeth and two other guys helped him down.

"It don't feel broken," he said as the two led him to the locker room.

The sun hadn't risen and I saw the moon trapped in the ice sheet of the gunnel. I started to sprinkle ice on the walkway but as I swung my arm I slid. I grabbed the safety chain but it's made of ice, too, and my glove ran off it. I moved forward and my foot came out from under me and I slid beneath the lower chain. My elbow hit the coaming and I thudded against the gunnel, one leg dangling over the edge of the barge. My arm and hip ached but what hurt most was my heart pounding in my chest. A wiry man with a dark hardhat offered his hand to me and we both carefully readjusted as I stood up.

"Go very damned slow," he advised.

"How many guys almost got killed out there this morning?" Larry asked everyone gathered in the locker room at lunchtime. "And it's still slick as shit on that metal."

He held up the same piece of paper he pulled from his pocket weeks ago and read the number on it out loud.

"That's our ticket. The union's never given a fuck but now we got some guys'll change that." He held the paper over his head.

"Vote 'em and they say they'll be here the moment we call." Everyone's face looked blank; we were exhausted.

*

Over the next two days the temperature moved toward forty degrees and the ice melted. It would be cold again on Saturday but I assumed we wouldn't work since the union election was Saturday.

"Wrong about that," Mueller corrected me. "They got us working all three shifts."

"What the fuck!?" I yelled and he put a hand on my shoulder.

"You know what the fuck. Everyone knows what the fuck."

Saturday turned out to be another frozen day with ice stacked thick over the surface of the world. On weekends the day shift began at five am rather than the usual seven am so the darkness lasted quite a while. Through the still moonlit hours we negotiated our paths across the frozen metal, slipped over the ice, and held our breath, but as soon as shift ended we busted ass to get to the union hall. We're pissed about how the union's conducting business: a lot of money was reported missing and there were rumors of that money going to cocaine for union officials. Some guys said they knew of union officials getting new pickup trucks from companies and had seen photos of prostitutes giving business agents blowjobs after lousy contracts were signed. Rumors, but whether or not they were true, a general distrust was in the air. The Rank-and-File slate had been getting a lot of support and seemed to have a real chance of winning.

On Monday morning the air was frosted and thick but everyone was cutting it up with snappy talk about the election. Tony ran up to me.

"I heard they won, I heard they won!"

"Who's 'they'"?

I crossed the railroad tracks and walked into the breakroom.

"Mueller and those guys from UPS."

I laughed. I saw Shaun and grabbed him by the shoulder. "You hear the news?!"

He grinned. "Hell, yeah! They fucking did it, my brother!"

We shook hands.

"Hey, Tapp," he said, extended his arms and waved them around. "All this bullshit... it's done."

"I'd advise you to take a day off," Mueller told me after the Monday-morning safety meeting.

"Can't afford to," I replied, "plus I'm ready to celebrate. Let them try any of their shit now. They know what's coming."

He rubbed his chin. "Yeah, they know what happened, but whether or not you can afford it, I'd get out of here for a bit. Company knows who supported who and, well, maybe there's a crane accident or something, you never know."

It was a totally paranoid warning, but I took a deep breath and thanked him and stayed home Tuesday.

*

I returned at dawn on Wednesday still excited until Mueller explained to me that the Rank-and-File victory had been retracted.

"They said it was an election discrepancy, some sort of miscount or misreporting or something. The independent slate won by 115 votes out of 18,000."

I spent the day in a daze, my head clogged with steam and gray, December clouds, enough to render me a ghost.

That afternoon, there was a commotion across the gantry crane tracks, the tracks that separated the two main lines of barges that ran through the shipyard. Men came off barges, crawled out from beneath barges and out of the sidebox ratholes, and they all gathered around the two-position barge, all of them looking up. I made my way down the icy ladder and onto the concrete. I pushed for a space in the crowd and I saw him. A fellow I didn't know sat on the iced-up gunnel, his leg dangling over the side of the barge, the nearest pole that held the safety chains wobbled in the air held aloft by the chains and free of its base, the weld line scraped against the skin of the barge. Another man slowly crept toward the injured man, navigating the ice and leery of the break in the safety chains. He was a First Responder and he yelled to someone in the crowd.

"Got a broken leg!"

The man in front of me turned around and I saw it was Ed, our union steward for that area. His lips were tight.

"It brings back memories."

*

The world warmed up considerably the following morning. A foreman approached me and told me I was moved to the two-position barge since the welder there broke his leg. I grabbed my equipment from the gang box and climbed the ladder on the two barge. On the way up a man extended his hand to me.

"I'm William," he said and smiled.

"Terry." I replied. William was a real presence; at least three-hundred and fifty, maybe four-hundred pounds, extremely dark skin, gold teeth in front.

"This is Bob," he said and pointed to the old man bent over to his side. Bob stood up when he heard his name. He struck me as the model for the perfect neighborhood gardener: smiling with small, round glasses – fitted with side shields to make them "safety glasses" – and white, curly hair, overalls, a flannel shirt.

"Bob's my buddy," William said and put his arm around Bob's shoulder, a gesture which dwarfed him.

As soon as I got to the top of the ladder William yelled out to me, "Hey, hey, Terry!" I looked down at him and he waved.

"You doin' ok?" he asked.

When I reached the gunnel I saw Shaun standing there and he gave me the sign for love.

"Hey, brother, looks like we're working together all the time from here on out."

I nodded my head.

"But you gotta see that old motherfucker's face every day now, too," he said and pointed to Lopp who sat on a plastic bucket and smoked a cigarette. Lopp flicked his cigarette butt at Shaun.

"Can we just get to work?" Kim asked as she walked by both of them. She looked at me. "You're working with all three of us now?" she asked, shook her head, and gave me a resigned grin.

Lopp and I dragged a load of six or seven arm-length ratchets and chains. Our job was to measure out the coaming of the barge, square it off and align it by cutting the brackets that held it up then weld them into straight positions. Lopp said we needed to start at the stern and work our way toward the rake so we took our tools to the stern and set them down. Lopp lit another cigarette as someone called out from below.

"Hey Lopp, hey Lopp! Hey Terry!"

We looked over the side of the barge and there was William who waved to us.

"How you doin'?"

Lopp put his hand on his forehead.

"That fatass. He kills me."

I shrugged. "He's just being friendly."

"He does this shit all day long," he groaned.

The next morning I climbed the ladder to the barge and then down into the cargo hull to get a welding line. The company tried to cut corners in every direction; there's one welding machine for each welder so if a machine's down, one guy's out of luck. He's got to find a machine somewhere in the vicinity and splice together enough weld line to reach his worksite. That can be a real, back-breaking hassle. That morning, though, I was lucky. I took the weld line and pitched it like a lasso over the chains running along the gunnel.

Atop the deck, Shaun unpacked the ratchets while beside him Kim gnawed on a cigarette's last hope.

"What's up with you?"

She explained that, after she had taken all the trouble of getting a weld line up to the deck and in place and attaching a whip to it and adjusting the machine, someone took her line when she turned her back.

"Who the fuck did that?" Shaun spat.

Kim bit down on her cigarette butt, didn't answer. Plain to Shaun and me the only line that led to Kim's area was being used by a thick man whose head and body reminded me of a spent bullet. Kim noticed us making this obvious connection and looked away.

Shaun and I together yanked the weld line and it flew out of Bulletman's hands. I unscrewed the whip from it as Bulletman ran up to us.

"What the hell do you think you doing?!"

"Keeping you from being a total asshole, you motherfucker," Shaun stated flatly.

I faced Bulletman squarely and let him see exactly what we were doing. He walked away, and searched for weld lines to tie to another machine.

"That's the type of back-stabbing motherfucker that works here," Shaun said. "This place is full of pricks like him."

*

A couple of weeks later I sat on a wooden bench in one of the locker rooms during lunch as around me many others sat and some stood, leaning against walls and lockers, all of us tired from work and cold, and without words. The holidays approached and the company pushed to get as much out of us as possible regardless of the safety of the pace. I held a book in my lap and sketched in it with a pen. My lines squirmed, meandered, promised shapes that almost hatched, and fell back. There was a peace among us, a certain peace only obtained from hard work and resignation. Near the center of the room a guy named Russell turned a scanner over in his hands and inspected the bottom. His dark blond hair was cut short, military-like and he bore an untrimmed yellow mustache. He shook his head in frustration.

"You know they got foreigners doing the weather broadcast these days?" He drew his lips tighter. "Just another job they take away from us."

Ed, the union steward for that area, leaned against the door and – for whatever reason, perhaps at Russell's comment, perhaps not – he chuckled. Russell reached behind him and put the scanner into his locker while pulling out another box.

Russell was constantly angry. He was angry that so many jobs had been and were being shipped out of the country, angry that so many friends and family were struggling so hard to make a living, angry at the company, angry at the union, angry at his back pain, angry that he was forty-one years old. To me, to all of us, Russell's rage was justified but we also knew that his daughter had been molested in day care, that he had pressed charges and taken the molester to court, that the man had received a sentence of several years for what he did, and Russell's daughter got counseling, and Russell was left with only one emotional setting.

"None of this is any good," he said and Ed laughed again.

Russell swiveled toward Ed.

"You think it's funny?"

"No, man, I'm just laughin'."

"I hurt." Russell lowered his head. "I hurt bad and I'm too tired to deal with the cold and this bullshit. I can't be treated like this any longer."

Ed had been leaning against the wall and he shifted and

walked toward Russell, but just as he started walking Russell opened the box on his lap and laying there on felt the color of ivy was a .45 caliber automatic pistol. Ed stopped and stared at the gun and, slowly, each head in the room pivoted to join him.

"I don't have anything," Russell whispered. "I need to get my share."

It seemed that Russell's gun was nothing but a hollow space, a center of a web, and we were the flies stuck to it with our nerves, stuck motionless.

Across the room, a fat, white man with a salt-and-pepper beard wearing striped overalls squeaked, "What're you plannin' on doin with that? Nobody in here has done you a wrong."

Russell raised his head.

"I wouldn't hurt none of you. I'm going to kill a foreman or maybe one of the assholes in the company building."

His words wandered the room for five or six seconds until they reached everyone and then we sighed and smiled.

"Hey," Ed yelled, "lunch is over!"

At the end of shift that day, we walked in two long lines to the gate. I looked at Ed.

"Anybody get shot today?"

He shrugged. "Guess not. I never heard anything about it. As he walked off he added, "Maybe next time."

*

Winter faded but slowly, in increments. The freezing days alternated with the merely cold and the rain returned. We thought nothing about this as we had become accustomed to walking away from dangerous working conditions, walking away together, and there was little the company could do. Or so it seemed. One afternoon in the first week of March, I worked with Shaun welding together the coaming on the position-two barge when the heavy sky began to fall, first in tiny, negligible drops then in a solid downpour, and we headed for the ladder to get off the barge. The downpour withdrew to light rain for a moment and standing on the platform at the top of the ladder was Alan, one of the foremen. Alan had a low-volume, high-pitched voice like a shy, preteen young lady but he was big and very fit and owned a martial-arts training school somewhere in the sticks.

"I've seen him kick," Shaun told me, "It's not pretty."

Alan folded his arms and stood at the edge of the ladder's platform closest to us and, as about seven or so workers approached, said "No one's going anywhere."

"It's raining," someone informed him of that obvious situation, "we'll get electrocuted."

Alan shook his head. "Rain idn't that bad and anyway, I just said no one's getting off this barge regardless."

We looked at one another and I could read the notion that passed between us: worried about our jobs if we took a wrench to Alan's head and potentially concerned about the front man in the line who might get his jaw broken by a karate kick before the rest of us could destroy Alan. Then I noticed something, or Shaun and I noticed it at the same time, since we both backed away from the confrontation with Alan and walked in the opposite direction. The platform leading to the ladder sat at the halfway point along the length of the barge and usually on starboard, and we walked from that point back to the bow then continued down portside to the stern and back around to the other edge of the platform and down the ladder. The entire time we walked, the remainder of our group faced Alan in a stare-down contest and moved only when they heard Shaun and me climbing down the ladder. Alan made an almost inaudible sound I remember a jackrabbit making when a friend of mine shot it with a dart. I glanced up to see Alan's face red and veiny and trembling with rage. Shaun caught it, too, and he started whistling a song, one I recognized immediately. I whistled along with him as we walked to the breakroom and through the door just as the downpour hit again.

Sunny Day
Sweepin' the clouds away
On my way to where the air is sweet
Can you tell me how to get
How to get to Sesame Street

Come and play
Everything's AOK
Friendly neighbors there
That's where we meet
Can you tell me how to get
How to get to Sesame Street.

Fucking idiot.

*

The next week winter returned with pain. The rain of the previous week froze and new ice and snow fell on top of it, a lot of snow. Everywhere was white. I worked amidst the awfulness of it until my clothes and gloves were frozen solid and a flock of images erupted in my skull that had to be released. I headed to a breakroom but it was full of loud, angry men and I craved quiet. I crawled back out into the icy attack and staggered in the snow and high winds around the barge. Wherever I went the winter rage found me. Finally I crouched alongside a vertical I-beam holding up one of the long, horizontal I-beams on which the barge sat and I took my small sketchbook and a pen from my work coat. I looked around me for a foreman, but they certainly wouldn't be found in that mess. As I looked I thought about the fact that, in most of the shipyard at that moment, we were caught up with work. We worked so hard and so fast that we had completed the current order of barges – at least the open-topped, hopper barges – ahead of time. But somehow this seemingly obvious and significant fact didn't affect the foremen's need to see me working, or for that matter, the whole, goddamned world's need to have me work. The company and the union must make me work, no matter what, no matter if work is finished, completed, unnecessary, wasteful, counter-productive or even deadly. I must be made to work, not because any work needs to be done, since clearly nothing needs to be done. This thing I need to do then couldn't be called "work" if by that term we mean something productive and necessary. What was required of me was a negative action, a doing that prevented a set of other actions from taking place. What could I have been doing? I could have been drawing, painting, writing, I could have been building something wonderful. I could have been building a house for someone without a home. I could have been repairing someone's roof who couldn't afford the repair work. All across Louisville, across Kentucky, across the United States and the entire globe, I had friends and acquaintances not working, but instead doing this other thing, this "unwork" that stood as an obstacle to positive, creative and necessary labor. I drew and wrote in the roar of winter and imagined what wasn't happening. I imagined another world entirely, swirling in a technicolor womb, its birth canal blocked by unwork.

*

Of course, unwork pays the rent. Unwork pays CitiGroup, CitiCorp, Citibank. Unwork was our real task and unwork seemed at its core to just a means of prevention of the emergence of the other world.

I couldn't draw with an icy welding glove on so that came off, as did my hardhat which I used for a stool. And there, in the face of the banshee wind and hard snow, I began to create. With my free hand I shielded the sketchbook from the snow which would have melted on it and weakened the paper and a thought occurred to me. According to some psychologists, certain things are necessary for creativity to occur. A certain set of needs has to be meet: we have to have enough to eat, for instance, an absence of physical pain, a modicum of stabilizing social contact, an emotional space relatively free from survival-oriented worries and so forth. But here I was, sitting on a hardhat in a blizzard, my fingers frozen, their tips cracked open with painful purple-red furrows, worried about getting caught and fired, worried about paying rent and having enough money for food and electricity, and yet from the end of my pen flew graceful and exquisite new beings, creation. And further, what would that seemingly standard understanding of human psychology have to say about the many men and women I'd met at the many horrible jobs I'd worked or "unworked," folks who stayed up late to draw or paint, folks who found or carried home scrap metal to cut and join together as sculpture when they had skipped eating that day, people who wrote poems and stories when their water or electricity were turned off, people who played music when they couldn't make rent? Our understanding of ourselves and how we function is a product of the study of the privileged – those wealthy enough or whose parents were wealthy enough not to be bothered by unwork or to be able to fully foist that burden on others, able to pay for therapy – and, on the other side, those folks on the desperate edge who can no longer get along at all in the society in which they live.

The overwhelming majority of people fall outside these two categories. We don't fit into the society in which we live: we are made to perform the tasks that keep the society running, made to do these things through laws and prisons and weapons and entertainment and education, but we haven't totally succumbed to these pressures. Instead we've learned a unique skill, a technique I would compare to the skill of a prehistoric human crossing a frozen tundra with a bundle of grasses and a burning ember inside them. We learned to keep the flame alive, the flame of our selves, our souls, despite the brutal demands of our masters. What our society calls "psychology" refers to an understanding of the inner lives of people with very few – if any – boots on their neck, or it refers to those who have crumbled. The other fields of psychology pertain to methods of manipulating us in cost-effective ways, often through implanting in us the means of self-manipulation and self-deceit. The majority of human experience lies outside these understandings.

*

The following day I understood what the commotion in the breakroom was about. Our foreman informed us that we weren't allowed to take any sort of break except to come off the job at lunchtime. There were no exceptions to this, no safety exceptions, no exceptions for the law which guaranteed us two fifteen-minute breaks a day in addition to our lunch break.

"We've already spoken with your union about this," Larry the foreman said, "and they're with us."

"We don't have a union!" someone shouted from behind me and Larry tilted his head and lifted his hands, palms up, as if to say "And...?"

For two days we worked, stunned and unsure about what to do, as we didn't stop to take a break in the morning or afternoon, as we worked at a breakneck pace and the foremen maintained a constant watch over us. Our lunchtime was shortened from thirty minutes to twenty as one foreman or another burst into our breakrooms and hollered for us to return to work, return to work, return to work. "They're serious about this shit?" I heard a number of people ask and yes, apparently they were very serious about working us to exhaustion. The only brightness to this situation was just that, the bright, sunny days as spring broke with temperatures in the high forties and no rain.

But the third day brought with it bloated, purple clouds and

heavy winds by nine o'clock. Around nine thirty in the morning
a torrential storm tore loose and for a mere few seconds I looked
at the men around me working and together we walked to the top
of the ladder. On the tops of ladders of barges and tankers across
the yard folks stood looking at one another as the rain beat onto
our coats and hardhats. "To hell!" an old man standing beside me
yelled and we barreled down the ladder to the breakroom. As I
came to the door of the breakroom, I saw Larry on the payphone
at the corner of the building. The cover above the phone was
cracked, much of the rain tore through and the blue light on the
cover dangled precariously.

"Don't worry!" he barked, "I'm calling the new guys at the
union hall! They'll take care of this!"

I ran over to him and told him to get out of the rain.

"We'll get fired!" he shouted and then his expression changed.
He beat the receiver against the body of the phone booth and
yelled, the rivulets of rain which squirmed down his face in the
blue aura made him look like a weeping angel. "It's not a real
number!" he cried.

Shaun bellowed, "Get out of the rain, you fucking loser!" and
ran into the breakroom.

I followed immediately.

The breakroom was full. Everyone in our area had walked off.
Mueller walked toward me and I stated this fact to him.

"That's not all of it by a mile," he smiled, "everybody's
walking off the job. A complete half of the damned shipyard is
walking off the job!"

I leaned back and pondered this development, for I hadn't
seen it coming though I suppose I should have. For a moment we
seemed to be weaker than I thought, we seemed to have caved in,
but a morning had shown us even stronger than I believed. A
group of foremen looked through the glass on the door in the
front of our breakroom then turned away. Somehow, I felt like we
had joined Dennis who found the possibility of freedom when

they suspended him. I pictured Dennis as our front man, leading us out of danger, running out of the shipyard, out of the world of welding, carpentry, fast food, data entry, retail, customer service, warehousing, and smashing through the back of the screen with red, tiny helicopters swarming around him as he soars beyond their control into an unimaginable, unimagined distance. A hero. Someone, a celebrity, maybe John Walsh, is pointing at the tear in the phony, video sky far above on the screen, the veins on his forehead bulging, deforming his face as he screams, his teeth exposed, "Go get him, America!"

*

The next Monday Shaun stood on the rake of the two-position barge and stared. I couldn't read his expression and, when he continued to stand still rather than grab his tools from the gang box, I approached him.

"You ok?" I inquired. "You seem out of it?"

He shook his head wildly.

"No, Tapp. I'm anything but ok."

I studied him as Lopp passed by.

"You get too drunk last night?" he asked and Shaun began to wander the deck.

"I gotta get out of here! I just gotta get out of here!"

Kim piped in, "We're behind again. There's no way they're gonna let you get out of that gate."

That day, Larry, our foreman, was absent and Rodney worked in his place. Rodney was even-tempered and generally agreeable, not only as a foreman, but as a person. He climbed the ladder and walked towards us and I thought Shaun planned to explain his situation to him, whatever his situation turned out to be. Instead, he ran to Rodney, grabbed his jacket and frantically demanded to be sent home. Rodney jerked back and stared at Shaun and tried to respond.

"Don't say nothing, man, just write me a slip! Write me a slip! I can't be here another second!"

Rodney took a pad of pink paper from his jacket and wrote an excuse for Shaun. Shaun grabbed it and ran to the ladder, across the gravel and into the locker room, then out of the shipyard.

"Boy's losing his goddamned mind," Lopp proclaimed.

Tuesday Shaun showed up for work on time, but said nothing for days.

*

A week or so later, on a cold afternoon, we finished work around two o'clock and there was nothing left to do, but Sloane found a task for us. The front and back coaming of the barges includes a set of letters and numbers used for identification of the vessel by the federal government and these numbers and letters are not merely painted onto the barge – which they are after the anti-rust paint is sprayed on – they are first written in relief with a welding rod. And that's what we were to do, write the identifying information onto some unattached sheets of coaming. The information was already written on the metal with soapstone. We were to take buckets, turn them upside-down and sit on them and slowly weld the soapstone lines into braille. Druck, who we called "Suck" on account of his behavior toward the foremen and company officials, came around with a metal tube of pink welding rods, a kind I had never seen before. I asked for the tub and read the safety warning on it. These rods were much more dangerous than the standard arc rods we used. These contained chromium and nickel compounds and required ventilator masks, even if we used them in the open air.

"I want a mask," I told Suck.

"Ain't gettin' one," he replied and walked away.

"Fuck it, then," I told the men around me and I turned a bucket over, sat on it, and did nothing.

A foreman from another area of the shipyard who had apparently been appointed to our area for that afternoon ran up to me and ordered me to get to work.

"Get me a mask!"

I showed him the warning on the tube and he began to yell. I yelled back and then sat on my bucket. "You're looking at getting suspended over this!" he hollered as he stormed off. Lopp looked over toward me when the foreman disappeared.

"Suspension means firing, you know that."

Shaun put down his welding hood and approached me.

"Tapp, I'm all with you on this bullshit, man. But we gotta work. So just do it, dude. I'd hate to see you get fired."

"Yeah, thanks, man, I'd hate that, too, but more than that, I'd hate to see me with chromeplated lungs."

He resumed welding and I sat on that bucket until the end of shift.

On top of the barge the next morning, Shaun leaned over the coaming. His head dangled and he coughed violently. He coughed on his hand and held it out for me to inspect. His skin was dotted with tiny drops of blood.

"What the hell is this?!"

Around me the others who had worked on the coaming the afternoon before all coughed, wheezed and gagged. I shook my head and said nothing. That afternoon Shaun explained to Larry that he was very sick and mentioned the pink welding rods.

"Well, we got a lot of men sick today," Larry informed him.

"Yeah, dude, everybody that welded with those little shit rods!"

Larry seemed at a loss for words. He frowned.

"You get better in time, son."

*

Spring unfolded on us with weeks of cobalt skies laced with

elegant clouds whose arms twirled in slow motion. Their size dwarfed me but it felt good, knowing we were part of a long tale with me only a single component, not unique and maybe not unfathomable. And that feeling brought me a certain hope, too, like noticing the monkey's thumb attached to my hand, signaling I hadn't yet ventured too far from home. There was a day not that long ago when the monkeys dreamed something bigger than going to work all day, every day, doing the same thing over and over simply to get some money. I pictured an ape exploring a tree still smoldering after a lightning strike. Breaking off a chunk of scorched wood, the ape makes a mark and pulls the beginning of a story out of itself. Like: one early afternoon I saw a young, red-tailed hawk rise from the trees to the east of the shipyard and glide along the river's edge beneath the clouds of spring. He passed me as I stood on starboard side facing the iridescent river, flew to the western end of the yard then turned around and came my way again. I took my sketchbook out of my hardhat and a pen from my work pants' pocket. What I drew was a dream-maker gesture, a single line, twisting and vibrating to life along the rim of the horizon.

Spring seemed to change the shipyard or to reflect a deeper change. We did our work, we worked hard but at a humane pace and the foremen left us alone, except for an occasional patrol to check on our work and of course the morning safety meetings.

At one of these meetings at the beginning of summer, the superintendent foreman informed us that we would be going to school one or two afternoons each week.

"Somethin' to help you," he said, "we call it QDC."

When he finished those words I noticed posters around the breakroom I'd never seen before, posters with shiny, gleaming graphics, the sort of multiple light rays and pornographic sparkles I'd seen on Baptist illustrations of Heaven. In the middle of the posters were the letters "QDC" in bright red. Sloane saw me inspecting a poster and he announced, "Q stands for quality."

He put his white hardhat on his head.

"I'm your QDC instructor, Tapp. We're meeting this afternoon."

I didn't care what D and C stood for.

At two that afternoon, a guy I'd never meet before – an orange hat like the rest of us, though – came around to tell us to meet in ten minutes inside a tiny, single-wide trailer sitting precariously on sinking cinder blocks in the mud very close to the river. Inside the trailer was a long table and many metal folding chairs. There was a shelf at the northern end of the trailer with a VCR on it connected to a television set below. Adjacent to the television set was a display easel on which was perched a large pad of paper and a set of charts, posters and other crap. Some of us unfolded chairs and slouched into them but others were forced to stand as there wasn't enough room for them. Sloane fiddled with the VCR for five minutes before he cussed and gave up.

"Ok, employees, we're concerned about quality out there. We want to make sure we get the best work out of you and deliver the best product to our customers."

He turned to the easel and picked up some charts.

"What we're gonna be doing is cross-checking. We're gonna help each other be the best we can be."

We looked at one another as he explained the QDC idea.

"The people who work beside you are gonna get trained on your job as well and they're gonna inspect your work and you're gonna do the same for them."

Paul pushed back from the table.

"We're going to spy on each other?!"

Sloane put the charts under his arm and waved his right hand.

"It's not spying, it's helping!"

He pulled the charts out again, stared at them, put them on the easel and turned to us.

"Like hell I'm spying on somebody!" an old man yelled.

Sloane put his hands on his hips.

"Goddamn it, nobody's spying! If the damned VCR worked you could see the film and understand it all better. I'm getting the thing fixed right now!" and he walked out of the trailer.

Several minutes later we passed around Sloane's charts and posters and a small instructor's manual he'd left on top of the television set. QDC was exactly what we thought; a way to get us to rat on each other. There was even a section in his manual on dealing with our negative feelings about ratting on our fellow workers. Another few minutes went by and we left the trailer, too, making our way back to our jobs.

The next day Sloane himself walked around the barge telling us that QDC training would be at two o'clock that afternoon. When he came to me, I took off my weld goggles and looked him in the eyes.

"I'm not going to be a snitch," I told him and the folks around me laughed and stated their agreement.

"Nobody is snitching on anybody," he groaned and walked away.

On the ground at the foot of the ladder I heard other people tell him the same thing.

At two o'clock we were back in the trailer but our mood was sour. Sloan messed with the VCR and no one spoke.

"I can't find the damned tape," he spat. "I'll be back!" And again he was gone.

But as soon as he left Samuel pulled the tape from his work coat and we all laughed.

"Rat-school instruction tape," he said and handed the tape to me. I opened the sliding glass of the trailer's window and pitched the tape into the weeds by the river and we went back to work.

A jittery older fellow with a toothpick in his mouth and a dirty gray mustache stormed past us as he left the trailer. "Yeah, fuck that there damned snitch-school bullshit," he snarled under his breath.

The posters in the breakroom stayed on the walls another

week or so, but no one ever mentioned snitch school again.

*

As we moved into autumn, we began to have more and more downtime, time that could have easily been filled with work if our pace of work was humane, but at the often dangerous speed the foremen tried to work us, gaps appeared in our shift. If we had worked at a safer, more humane speed, we could have gotten the job done and finished it for the same amount of money given all the overtime the high productivity schedule required.

I took advantage of these dead time zones and smuggled in a brand new sketchbook along with a couple of new books to read. But unfortunately, with all the downtime hitting us, my spots for reflection and drawing were becoming occupied. I walked along the row of barges closest to the river and noticed an opening in the corrugated steel sheeting in the front of a small white building, or rather, something closer in size to what I would call a large shed. I looked around and saw no one looking at me and I pulled back the sheeting and ducked inside. The steel sheet, it turned out, covered a sliding metal door I had never seen and inside the shed were two stacks of old bricks and what appeared to me to be the core of an engine, its exterior painted white. Gauges popped out of the sides of the engines and on top as well and a goopy, red fluid dripped off it. The goop – which I took to be something like transmission fluid – puddled on the floor. I walked toward the back of the shed and around the giant motor and I saw that, due to a slant in the ground on which the shed sat, the red liquid puddled at ten inches high or more. Black rat corpses and bugs floated in the crimson slop but sitting in the middle of the lake was a treasure: a wooden bench with legs long enough to keep it several inches above the slime. I piled bricks in a walkway of increasing height and made my way to the bench. Just as I did, the engine came to life in a nearly ear-splitting roar which lasted for all of thirty seconds and I offered thanks for this. No one would bother to brave that noise, the red glop, the rat bodies and insects, just to find me. I pulled out my sketchbook and began to draw and dream.

*

The company negotiated a contract with the Vane Brothers, a group looking to build ocean-going barges, ships even more massive than those we normally constructed. The contract was for an enormous amount of money and would keep us in work for quite a while. That was good as we were coming to the end of several large orders of hopper barges, the open-topped sort. And as we approached the end of that order, we kept hitting spots of truly dead time, time which, despite their best efforts and regardless of the push to overwork us, the foremen could barely fill.

Larry returned to work late that fall. He'd been gone for two months or more, ever since the union election, and no one had any information about him. When he reappeared he was much heavier and spoke little. Our union steward said Larry had a breakdown and had been institutionalized. He lived with his parents now. He was forty-five years old. I watched closely to see if I could find a difference between the before-breakdown Larry and the after-breakdown Larry. I assumed his mental collapse took place outside of work – maybe after work or on the weekend or between shifts even – because I hated the thought that I could have been looking him straight in the face and inside he was disintegrating like a dandelion in the breeze. What had I seen or failed to see?

I disliked Larry's boastful naiveté but otherwise he was pleasant company. He played bass and used to play covers in a local band, but there wasn't much demand for it around Louisville, certainly no demand that paid. Larry had a wife and a couple of kids to support so he became a flatwelder at the shipyard.

Flatwelders don't move much. They use a long and thick welding rod that doesn't require you to weave the liquid metal together or stack it. You just touch the rod to the surface and the metals blend in a bright pool the size of the tip of your thumb. Flatwelders stand or sit with one arm stretched out and glare at that pool for eight or more hours a day as the rod slowly burns away. One old man told me that when he was a flatwelder, he would see the little pool of metal all day for ten or twelve hours, then go home and dream of it all night.

"It turned all my days and nights and weeks even into one horrible afternoon."

At lunch one day last year, Larry told us a story about what happened to him three years back.

"I was flatwelding on top of a barge," he said, "when somebody tapped me on the shoulder to let me know it was time for lunch. I started to walk down the ladder but all I could see was that glowing spot and I ended up falling. Broke my hip in five places when I hit the ladder and bounced off the concrete." He paused, choked up for a second, then roared, "Here's a crocashit for you! The insurance barely covered anything. It's an 80/20 plan and they backed out of half of their share! This shipyard's chartered in the state of Indiana and in Indiana they got the laws so as you can't sue your employer! You know how much those surgeries cost?! I got pins all in me now. I'll be paying on it the rest of my life!" He yanked a cigarette from his shirt pocket. He pulled a lighter from his pants pocket and tried unsuccessfully to light the cigarette. "Hell, I couldn't even fuck my wife for months." Someone threw him a pack of matches. He lit the cigarette and drew on it. "Here's another thing: the only lawyer I could afford told me he didn't even know who I could sue. Not my employer, not the insurance company, not the doctor, not the foreman, not the ladder manufacturer. I guess I could sue one of you or maybe myself."

Before he disappeared into the institution, Larry worked overtime almost every day. He had to work that much to pay for the medication he needed related to his injury and for the medication his daughter needed for her epilepsy. After he returned, he showed the foremen a note that instructed them to send him home after eight hours every day, regardless of overtime. I asked him how he was doing when we walked beside one another after shift was over.

"I know you're not getting the overtime you need," I mentioned.

"No, but I'm okay now," he told me, smiling, and I saw that his eyes were unfocused. "My parents take care of me and I'm on a lot of meds. We got a new contract coming up and I think they're gonna increase the insurance and that'll help me and my parents out a lot."

Larry obviously needed help but our insurance didn't cover therapy or even a prescription for pills. The parent company, not CitiGroup but American Commercial Lines, the one in between CitiGroup and us that owned the shipyard, did provide a short-term counseling service and, if they approved you, you would receive up to seven half-hour sessions with a human being along with the possibility of a prescription.

Several weeks later, Larry vanished again and no one has seen him since.

I asked a couple of Larry's friends about him one afternoon on the way out of work. One guy shook his head and gestured like he was swatting away a fly.

"Long gone," he said.

"He was having a lot of problems, I know that," I added, "and all they gave him was a bunch of pills, and he had to pay for those."

The other guy laughed bitterly.

"He oughta be glad he got them damn pills."

He pointed to an area down the street from the shipyard.

"I live right over there. There's a guy works at the carpentry shop at the shipyard. My nextdoor neighbor. Hung himself last month. Whatever was eating him, they wouldn't even shove a handful of antidepressants down his throat to give him a break."

"Damn," I said, "that's hideous."

"Yeah, his brother found him hanging from a ceiling fan. His feet was twisted around his legs and his face looked like it was made out of dough and somebody'd squeezed it in their fist."

He clenched his teeth and held his fist out in front of him. We three walked out of the gate in silence.

"At least he doesn't have to work here anymore," he admitted as a consolation.

*

That weekend we worked only half of a day Saturday, a chilly, azure-sky, late-autumn day, and I was excited to go home to my child and my paintings. I packed my work leathers in my locker as someone's scanner broadcast the weather report. It was a phoneme-generated computer voice and it told of a gorgeous day and a repeat of it on Sunday. I walked around the lockers to see Russell staring at the scanner.

"What kind of accent is that?!" he growled. "Go back to your own goddamned country and let an American have that job!"

*

The company finally pulled in new orders for a number of barges and tankers and we were busy and we did our jobs, but we fought the company on their continual efforts to work us into the ground, to speed us up past the point of safety. Not only did we not want to die, but we also understood that any extra effort we gave worked against us. We seemed to have gotten very strong, to be able to shut down an area or even half of the shipyard when necessary. Life began to feel like a battle once more.

One promise the new crew of union officials, who had been the somewhat lower level of incumbents, made to us was that the progress of the negotiating committee for our upcoming contract would be transparent. In the past, the union and the company had hashed out an agreement and presented it whole hog or nearly-finished and we had little say about contract proposals. This was supposed to change, and it didn't. We received no news whatsoever about the contract deals, and we were upset about that fact. We knew the company wanted things from us beyond all they already wanted. There was the Vane Brothers contract, for instance, which would make the company a lot of money if things went well. We alerted people about the problems with the negotiating committee through the newsletter, we smuggled it in and the foremen tried to confiscate the copies, as usual.

After the four-day weekend of the Thanksgiving holiday and before the same of the Christmas holiday, an air of good feeling fell over us. We had some control over our lives at work, even if our lives outside of work were no more in control given the low pay, but the company appeared to have crawled off our backs for the moment. The union crowd got the election results they wanted, one way or another. The big boats were getting built as required and we were certain that this upcoming contract would contain some significant pay raises among other good things. There was a lot of work to be done and we showed that not only were we capable trade workers, but we were good union people too, in the real sense of union.

On a midweek morning freezing rain fell hard. It had been falling that way before dawn and it showed no signs of stopping. The voodoo of the weather forecaster agreed and we expected to be sent home shortly. It would be Christmas soon and we were tired. No one even pulled his or her equipment out of a locker, but instead we talked, played cards, read the newspaper, and I sketched, as the rain intensified. Sloane entered the main breakroom for our area, looked around and left. I saw him, but no one else seemed to pay him any mind. He shot back in within minutes and this time, he flung the metal doors open.

"What the hell are you men doing?!" he shouted and everyone shut up. "We have work to do, gentlemen!" and he pointed to the flat, purple morning and the roaring rain.

"Fuck you!" someone yelled and he was joined by others until the room sprung up in a chorus of rage.

Sloane yelled back and was joined by several other foremen. We pounded the metal tables and hollered and the foremen left, but Sloane, on his way out, bellowed, "Every single one of you is suspended!"

Mueller ran into the breakroom as the foremen left and he sat beside me. He was smiling.

"Anybody get up from here?" he asked and I told him they hadn't. "Nobody in the next breakroom or the locker rooms obeyed," he chuckled.

A fellow I didn't know entered the breakroom and parked himself with us.

"Same up at the other end, too," he told Mueller.

Mueller leaned over to me. "That's the whole damned yard," he grinned.

I laughed and Shaun, who had been standing behind me laughed, too.

"Hell, yeah!" he joined in.

"So that's a yard-wide screw you?" someone asked and before anyone could answer a union steward shoved the breakroom doors wide open and said, "Let's be getting out of here! No one's working in this shit today!"

We grabbed our things and headed to the nearest gate. The gates wouldn't open unless their clocks read beginning or end of shift or unless one of the security crew pressed some button or another. The line was huge and I looked eastward to see another line forming at the next gate.

"Open the damned thing!" someone yelled and a dozen voices immediately joined him. The rain pounded us as we waited and, just as I thought we were going to have to change our strategy, the gates opened and we flooded out.

I climbed into my van, closed the door, and Paul knocked on my window.

"That's yard-wide!" he shouted. I rolled down my window. "Yard-wide!"

"Merry Christmas," I wished him and I leaned out the window. We embraced and I felt him shake from the cold rain and from joy.

*

Paul came to my aid at the end of the winter, when the company decided to institute a new drug-testing program. Instead of a foreman hauling us off to be drug-tested, we were to do this to ourselves. If we suspected that our fellow worker was under the influence of some safety-compromising substance (not a safety-compromising influence like work stress, pressure to speed up work, harassment or straightforward safety-compromising situations like faulty equipment or being made to work in unsafe conditions), we were to notify a foreman or security person and that worker would be hauled out for testing. Drug-testing was a form of suspension since you were required to wait until the lab reports returned before you could return to work. If the lab reports showed there was something in your blood the company didn't approve of (not simply something toxic since the company approved of profitable toxic substances), you would be assigned to drug treatment or rehab before you could return to work. We were outraged at this program which was clearly yet another way to turn us against one another and into snitches.

On the other hand, as I mused at one of our meetings, if the laboratory report came back clean, the company was on the hook to reimburse you for the time you were off which could be a few days or even a week. That reimbursement included any possible overtime you might have been offered. When I mentioned this at the meeting, everyone understood that we were potentially in for some paid vacation. Our alternate vacation program took off and we began to rat out each other every day, clearing this with one another first to make sure that person's lab work would in fact show no problems.

I was assigned to a new work area under a foreman – Scott – who seemed, against the requirements the company placed on him, to be a nice fellow and to have our safety and welfare in mind, unlike most of the other company people. And that was unfortunate for me. When my turn at drug vacation arrived, Paul told Scott I smoked a joint in the locker room and that I was still in the locker room, hiding and stoned. I sat on a bench and waited for Scott. I heard him enter the room and I faced the wall rather than turn to greet him. He sat beside me and stared at me for a moment while I continued to contemplate the white-tile wall.

"Terry, I need you to come to my office, alright?"

He put his hand on my shoulder.

I let him repeat himself then I acted as if his words had just been delivered to my brain and that drop-off surprised me and made me stumble as I stood up and followed him to his office.

"Look, man," he sighed, "we all have problems and this is totally out of character for you, but I heard you were getting high in the locker room, smoking up on the job."

I stared blankly at him and he reached into the drawer of his desk.

"I'm gonna give you a break," he said and vaguely smiled. "This is an excuse to go home. You only got an hour left on shift. Just head out the gate and be safe. You'll only lose a little bit of pay for the day but you get the chance to come back tomorrow and start fresh, ok buddy?"

I almost broke my act out of anger but I stayed in role.

"Um, thanks."

I took my little do-gooder excuse and damnit-damnit all the way out the gate.

*

Our contract with the company was expiring and we were going to vote on a new contract, one that, we hoped, would be good given the strength we'd displayed: we had stood by one another and we understood what we were capable of doing, and so did the company. The contract vote was Sunday morning, April 29th, and the union hall was packed. We sat on metal, folding chairs spread in rows radiating outward from the stage in the hall's downstairs auditorium. On our right union staff had placed a handful of voting boxes on long legs with curtains on the boxes' open side lined with faded red, white and blue stripes. I brought my son with me, who was a toddler, and I exchanged a few corny jokes with the folks near me. All the faces I saw looked hopeful.

Then we looked at the contract. It was a stapled collection of pages whose cover read, "Last, Best and Final Offer." "Final Offer" is a legal term used by negotiators to signal that, should the offer – the contract – be rejected, that rejection would qualify as an automatic strike vote. But this final offer was actually the first offer for us, our first glance at what the company was proposing, and it was terrible. The pay raise was negligible, the insurance costs would eat that increase and more. The contract wasn't a typical three-year contract but a five-year contract, one extending through the period the company needed to craft that series of very profitable, ocean-going vessels. That extension would give the company a legally-guaranteed stable period with its "workforce." Item by item the contract was junk but, to add to the insult, there was a clause in the contract granting the union the power to alter the contract in accordance with the company's wishes without the consent of the union's members!

But our mood was good and our vote was overwhelmingly "No." After we voted, the president of the union, who had been present to oversee the vote, informed us that we were now on strike and a picket schedule would be posted in the main hallway of the union building later that day. As a group we were fine with this. We'd been working our asses off and could use a day or two of vacation. We were sure any strike would be very brief given that the company was working on that ocean-going deal and representatives from the group commissioning the boats would be touring the shipyard that week when they came into town for the Kentucky Derby. We had an ample strike fund, though the fund only provided a portion of our regular income and that was a low bar to begin with. I shook a few hands, took my son home, changed his diaper, and relaxed.

That evening three friends stopped by and we drank beer and talked. I felt great. I was looking forward to a couple of days of rest, of painting and spending time with my son, catching up on sleep, reading, and a thousand other things that got pushed aside by work and couldn't possibly fit into the tiny window of human life opened up by the flash vacation provided by our rejection of the final offer. As we talked my phone rang. On the other side was a union representative who told me that we were in fact not on strike and that I would need to show up on time for my regular shift which, in this case, would be at dawn the coming morning.

"Like hell!" I told her, "We voted on a final contract and we're on strike. The union president said he'd put up picket schedules."

She again claimed we were not on strike and informed me that not showing up on time and ready for work would mean discipline from the union.

"What does that mean?" I asked and she dodged me by repeating herself like a machine.

"So what are you going to do?" one of my friends asked.

"I voted," I told her, "I'm on strike."

"What about 'discipline'?" she asked.

I shrugged, then turned to my wife. "I'm going down there at dawn. We'll hide you outta sight with a camera and you keep the car running. When they discipline me, take pictures and head out of there, ok?"

All three friends wanted to come along though one had a mother sick with cancer who needed his attention. I shook my head.

"If you go," I said, "you're going to face discipline, whatever that means. And worse than that, you're gonna have to be at the shipyard's main gate at five thirty in the morning, way out of your beauty-rest zone."

They insisted on joining me.

That night I couldn't sleep thinking about what I needed to do and whatever I was going to face as "discipline." Around midnight I drove to the shipyard to size things up in my brain. On gate one, a smaller gate, a handful of folks gathered in a parking lot and I stopped to see what they were planning. I pulled in just as a cop car arrived.

"You gotta leave, gotta go," he told the group.

"We're on strike," someone said and the cop repeated himself. Everyone looked tired and confused. I asked the man who replied to the cop what he intended on doing and he had no answer.

"Well, I'm striking," I informed him and he wished me luck.

That was the third shift coming in to work. That meant there'd be folks in the shipyard when I arrived at one of the big gates at dawn.

I was totally unprepared for a strike. The union was supposed to have signs printed and a picket line coordinated but, since our union was working with the company or at least not working with us, we were required to pick up our own school supplies. It was one in the morning. I drove to a big box store out on a highway and found it closed. After another forty-five minutes of wasting time and gas, I headed home and managed to sleep for a fitful couple of hours.

*

My wife and I picked up our bleary-eyed friends at five am and we made it to gate eight by five thirty. No one was there. My two friends and I walked to the street while my wife pulled the car to the side of a small restaurant where a bit of tree cover shielded the car. As we stood on the sidewalk, I realized we could have easily been taken as anything other than strikers. I never picked up any poster board or anything for us to write on. But I brought a handful of fat-tipped, black markers and I saw some cardboard in the dumpster in the workers' parking lot. We took the cardboard and wrote messages like "Our contract sucks!" (and on the back, "So does Zuckerman," the president of our local), "Drink Milk," "Fuck this Union," and so forth. We didn't want to simply write that we were on strike since, legally, we weren't on strike. As we walked back and forth along the stretch of sidewalk in front of gate eight, cars began to honk at us and their drivers raised their fists in support. Dilapidated cars and trucks began to fill the parking lot behind us and to our left, while folks with lunchboxes stood along the entrance watching us, not budging. A heavy-set fellow approached me and asked what the hell these people were doing walking around with signs, people he'd never seen before, people who didn't work at the yard, outsiders. I told him they were people braver than he was, people doing what he should be doing. He looked around then asked me where I'd gotten the signs and I pointed to the dumpster. He returned with some cardboard and I handed him a fat-tipped marker. Other folks joined him. No one entered the shipyard at gate eight that morning.

Around nine am I was getting tired. The crowd along gate eight had grown to hundreds of people. Some brought their own, handmade signs attached to sticks or boards. Some brandished dumpster-material signs like those my friends and I used. I decided to head home for a bit and grab some sleep. My wife had already headed back.

*

Right after I left, the workers who had arrived at work on third shift or accidentally come to work on one of the other gates on first shift, without realizing we were keeping the strike alive in spite of our union, tried to get out of the shipyard but were trapped by the turnstiles that only opened at the beginning and end of shifts and by the fencing around the shipyard. Many clung to the fencing, rattling it, some halfway climbing it, yelling in support of their fellow workers. Who said this is a permissible way to live, imprisoned by chain link simply because someone claims to own something, in this case a company, a shipyard? As a friend said to me regarding ownership and what it entails, a friend long dead: So what? You can simply claim ownership and all the rights it gives you but when your ownership prevents me and the people I love and value from fully living the one, unique life we have, I can just as easily deny your ownership and claim back all the rights my rejection gives me. These people were caged like animals.

When lunch arrived the folks trapped inside the shipyard were set free and they jumped into their trucks and cars and hauled ass to the union hall knowing full well the union leadership would have to be on their side this time, this one, single, significant time. And at the union hall they were told by the president of the union that a clerical mistake meant they were, in fact – in solid, screw-you, biblical fact – forced to get on their knees and obey what the union and the company had typed onto a sheet of paper. They were not allowed to strike, vote or no-vote. According to the conditions agreed to by the union and the company, the union was supposed to notify the company within sixty days that they were interested in negotiating a new contract. If the union didn't notify the company about this obvious fact, the contract would be extended by a year. The union claimed they had forgotten to notify the company on time: in fact, they notified the company of this exactly one day after the deadline, so, apparently, they had been negotiating in bad faith all along, with full knowledge that their efforts could have no impact. Either way, we workers were one-hundred-percent bound and delivered if we played by the law. But we were making a new decision. We decided to no longer play by the law and so our future could not be found typed on any sheet of paper or any screen.

Everyone turned their backs on the union hall and drove away, but instead of heading home, they headed to the shipyard and there, on the mile and an eighth of street north of the shipyard, they brought out lawn chairs and coolers and tables and posted signs along the fencing. We were ready to do anything but crawl back through those gates. The unofficial, illegal strike – the wildcat – was underway.

The police appeared almost immediately, setting up shop right across from us, riding back and forth along the picket line, giving off waves of tension and surveillance.

That afternoon I posted news about the strike – which most of us still assumed would be very brief – on the internet and responses were beginning to come through. There was a lot of well-wishing from within the United States but at least as much from other countries. Many of those from other countries who emailed in response to my announcement of the strike expressed surprise that anything even remotely like an uprising would take place in the United States. This reaction bothered me, in part because the history of the US is rich with uprising from the nation's origin onward and also in part because surprise was a legitimate response to an uprising given the behavior of the people residing in the US today.

I drove back to the shipyard that afternoon and walked the length of the picket line. A mile and an eighth length of angry, frustrated and somehow hopeful people. There were now signs all over, cardboard, some sheets, a lot of poster board. Some of these signs expressed anger about the so-called "clerical error" that, according to the union, had put us in this place. Some of the signs asked for honks of support. Some stated that we were doing this for our children's future.

I talked to many people along that line and they all expressed their expectation they'd be presented with a better contract than the one we rejected. Aside from the spin the union put to the public, and the fairytales we wished were true, we knew they'd screwed us; that they worked with the company, and we already knew the company was against us. But we had shifted the game board by staying on the street rather than complying for no matter how efficiently you've screwed a group of people (your "workforce"), how do you control them when they're all sitting on the sidewalk playing cards, drinking beer and giving you the finger?

This was a barbeque, a party, and like at most good parties, we drank, told stories and didn't sleep. That spring night, as I stood among the laughter and bullshit on the street and looked around me, I met someone. But the encounter was shaped differently than typical encounters which, from my perspective, always begin from the periphery of my experience and move closer. This began from the interior and moved toward the periphery, a shape of things happening I'd only known to occur when I was deep into a painting or drawing. My chest expanded and my breathing grew troubled like a great thing spread its wings inside me. I recognized this sensation as a hatching, an awakening among new, long-lost kin. I looked around and witnessed this happening to others around me, the evidence being an added brightness that motivated their faces. This wasn't something I saw with my eyes. I realized there's a kind of significant light you can only understand when you defy a wicked power.

*

Early Tuesday morning the Quick Mart across the street from the shipyard opened and the owner invited us to get cups and take as much water as we needed. He also allowed us the use of his store bathroom which was helpful. I got a cup of coffee from him and walked back to the picket line.

Around eight o'clock or so, I stood in front of gate five, essentially the main gate, when the president of the company drove hurriedly into the yard barely giving us time to jump out of the way. He paused and waved to us when he was safely in the shipyard. Shortly after he arrived a cop car pulled into one of the designated parking spots. Patrol cars had been circling like barracuda all Monday but this seemed different. And apparently it was. An officer got out of the car and followed the president into the building. He stormed back out almost immediately and drove off.

"I think that was the chief of police," a fellow striker told me.

Whether or not that was true, an hour or so later a patrol car coasted down the street in front of the shipyard. The cop looked long at us as he passed then stuck his arm out of the car window, his hand in a fist. "Fuck 'em!" he yelled and we applauded, shouting the same back to him, to the sky, to the company president and any administrators inside. "What the hell?"

A short man I'd never seen before stepped out of the crowd and spoke.

"The police chief said half of their calls come from JeffBoat and the cops're sick of their bullshit. JeffBoat's on their own."

The police in Jeffersonville had been working for two years

without a contract and suffered from low wages and long hours much like us. All Tuesday and every day thereafter, patrol cars cruised by slowly, the officers raised their fists, honked and shouted support.

Later Tuesday afternoon three cars and an SUV pulled into the parking lot by the small restaurant across from the shipyard. They were the typical, beaten-up rides most of us drove. From them men and women emerged and they brought folding tables on which they placed coolers and bags that turned out to contain sandwiches and fried chicken and soup. I walked over to get some soup as I hadn't eaten in the excitement. No one spoke of what was happening; instead we talked about the sort of food we preferred; turkey or bologna, peanut butter with jelly or with honey or simply by itself, white bread versus rye or wheat or potato bread. We joked a bit and then settled into eating the simple, wonderful lunch we had been given. The only significant detail I took from this moment was that no one seemed to know these people. They saw what was occurring and they helped us. This happened again and again throughout the week.

I drove home briefly and checked my email and saw that there were hundreds more emails directed to us, the workers at JeffBoat, encouraging us, congratulating us, wishing us luck. I printed some of these out and drove back to the strike line.

Somewhere near the middle of the mile and an eighth of the picket line, a semi-truck had parked. The driver was making a delivery of bottles of water to a Walmart when he heard news of the strike. He stopped, opened the loading door of his truck, and began unloading cases of water for us. A number of us joined him and stacked the cases around the back of the Quick Mart. He shook many of our hands and thanked us, then departed.

Folks began to pass around a petition to decertify the Teamsters as our union. The petition received most of our signatures but the process of decertification is complicated. We have to petition the National Labor Relations Board to conduct a decertification election and there is only a thirty-day window of time available for voting, and that window exists only before a contract expires. Once a contract is agreed to by the company and the union, the union can't be decertified and, given the situation we were in, it was unclear if our contract had expired or simply rolled over. On top of that, if the decertification election was conducted, we could just as easily wind up with no union at all and, in that case, the company wouldn't even have that small incentive to obey any safety regulations or precautions whatsoever. As usual, following the law meant nothing more than accepting defeat.

But we'd become the union. We had acted in the manner and spirit of an actual union, so whether or not we were protected by any legallyrecognized entity, we could take care of ourselves.

*

A May Day rally was taking place in downtown Louisville that afternoon and some of the organizers asked me to speak at it, on the part of the JeffBoat wildcat strikers. The rally was huge but the number of participants was met with double that of police officers. The police brought horses, motorcycles, patty wagons and small, armored vehicles, and surrounded the park. Some people played music and others spoke about things such as job loss, poverty in the community, and so forth. Before I took the mic, I told my friends that several labor organizations would surely be attending. I had spoken with them, in particular Jobs With Justice, whose work I respected. I wanted to wait to speak until they arrived. My friend Barry, a long-time labor and HIV/AIDS activist in Kentucky, finally pulled me aside.

"They're not coming. No organization is coming."

I told him they had emailed me about it and it was definite.

"They money from Local 89, Terry. It's an illegal strike. No one is coming."

We stopped by my place briefly and I printed up more emails which kept pouring in. That night, I began to read the emails to the crowd at gate one and they were stunned that people in Brazil and Russia were aware of what we were doing and were saluting us, thanking us.

"Why would anybody in South America care if a bunch of hillbillies are getting shit on?" a lady asked me. I answered that what we have to deal with most people across the planet are dealing with, some a bit better, some much worse.

I walked toward the next gate and read more emails to those sitting on chairs or standing in between these points and my voice was growing hoarse from shouting and talking. A bald man I recognized from the machinists' crew handed me a megaphone and I thanked him. Before I arrived at gate five, another fellow asked if I'd like a platform, meaning the bed of his pickup truck, from which to read and I gladly accepted his offer. For hours throughout Tuesday night, we toured the gates and anywhere people were gathered. He stopped the truck and I stood in the back with the megaphone reading, letting people know that there were many, many others watching us and supporting us. Those people on that picket line listened, many of them puzzled, incredulous, or even astonished to learn that anyone gave a damn about our lives, but all of them seemed touched and transformed by that awareness.

The sun shot bolts of pink and crimson and yellow against the sky at dawn Wednesday morning and I realized its beauty affected me all the more due to my lack of sleep. Few of us were able to rest. I saw Tony walking along the street and winding through groups of strikers, his mouth slightly open. He seemed delirious, as much if not more so than the rest of us. I approached him.

"You alright, man?"

He shook his head and stretched his arms out wide. "I feel the presence of the Lord here," he exclaimed and others around us nodded in agreement.

*

Later that morning a very clean, scarlet pickup truck crept east down the street in front of the shipyard then suddenly spun southward and barreled into our picket line at gate five, almost hitting several of us. We dove out of the way to make an opening for the truck and, as soon as it passed through the gap, the driver hit her brakes and jumped out. Her name was Angela, a steel fitter from the hopper line, and she stepped up to me, put her face inches from mine and started screaming. The others on that section of the picket line, some of them picking themselves up from where they jumped, surrounded us.

"You lazy hillbillies!" she screamed. "Get your asses outta the way! And while you're at it, why don't get back to work?!"

She threw her arms around her, her hands balled into fists. A crane operator who always seemed to wear a red shirt jumped across the hood of her truck and stood behind her.

"You wanna fight?! You almost ran us over!"

He was ready to grab her. I yelled for him to back up and I noticed that others had adopted the same stance and the same expression. They wanted to pummel her, as did I.

"We have a good reason to be out here," I told her.

Someone behind me yelled, "Yeah, we're tired of being broke and working our asses off to get there!"

She snarled at us. "You're all broke 'cause you live paycheck to paycheck! Get the hell away from me!" and we backed up to let her step into her truck and drive into the yard.

I didn't understand her response that morning or what reasoning lay behind her actions. As we discussed the incident on the picket line, I learned that she was a fundamentalist Christian and lived an hour southward with her long-term girlfriend. None of that made sense to me.

*

Wednesday afternoon I stopped by my house to find three letters had arrived, one from the president of JeffBoat, the second from the president of the Teamsters local, and the third from the Industrial Workers of the World (IWW). I opened the letter from the IWW first, which turned out not to be an official letter from the IWW but a personal letter from the IWW General Secretary-Treasurer, Fred Chase. Fred was interesting to me as he had a long history of involvement in political life, from union-organizing to setting fire to an Army draft office during the Vietnam War and spending time in jail for it. I sat hard into the chair in the front room to read the letter and I realized I hadn't slept since Monday morning and I could barely hold my head up. Opening Fred's letter took almost more effort than I could muster. Fred wrote that he was reading the news about the wildcat strike and he was overjoyed. It was the first of May and the first May of the new millennium and there was a large strike, a wildcat strike, in the heart of the United States.

"What you people are doing makes me very happy. I know you're supporting a family and no money's coming in. I hope this helps."

I looked in the envelope and found a check for what amounted to a week's pay. Exhaustion and relief overcame me and I cried and fell into a deep sleep.

When I awoke later that evening, I pulled out the other two letters and read them. The letter from JeffBoat's president read:

May 2, 2001
Dear JeffBoat Employee,
The purpose of this letter is to fill you in on what's going on at JeffBoat. I have enclosed a summary of the proposal you voted last Sunday.

I hope everyone understands the situation with the

picketing. The current contract remains in effect under the renewal clause on page 48. The contract will remain in effect for one year unless a new contract is voted for by a majority of employees. Under Article XX of the contract, any strike during the existing contract is illegal. We want everyone to return to work so that the needs of our customers can be met, which protects the jobs of those employees who want to work.

The Company has not taken disciplinary action against any employee. Some of you may fear you've already lost your job, either by being fired or by pointing out. That's not true. Your job at JeffBoat is waiting for you and the offer is still on the table.

We are asking all employees to report immediately to work on their regular shifts. We are requiring that all employees report by the start of their regularly scheduled shift on Monday, May 7th (third-shift employees report at 10:30 pm on Sunday night May 6th). For all employees who report to work as scheduled, there will be no penalties for being absent this work week. Any employee who does not report by this deadline will be subject to discipline up to and including discharge.

We all want JeffBoat to be a good place for you to work and to provide for your families. I look forward to working together to build a stronger JeffBoat.

Thanks,

Robert W. Greene

President

I had never received a letter from the president of the company before, but I had read the one, single issue of the company's newsletter which featured him and it stated he was a great guy so I knew that much. I also knew he was a very busy man, since he had told us so at a safety-awards speech he made a year before. At that speech he complained that we were not working hard enough, not working fast enough. He said that he was a very busy man and it was unfortunate that he had to stop what he was doing for weeks at a time to sit in front of the enormous window in his office and watch us for eight hours, for our entire shift, day after day, and witness us not working fast enough. This upset him but now he wasn't upset at us; now he was my penpal and I wrote him back with a letter that I took to a copy center, printed in large quantity that night, and brought back to the picket line. It read:

May 3, 2001

Dear Bob:

The purpose of this letter is to fill you in on what's happening on the street in front of JeffBoat.

I hope you understand the situation with the picketing. You pay us half of the industry standard wage. You try to force us to work in the rain. You try to make us work when there's lightning overhead. You waste our time with your petty little jackshit "safety requirements" to make sure your ass is covered for the insurance reps but you won't do a damn thing to really ensure our safety. You drag us to your drug tests like we're puppies that pissed on the carpet. You work us like slaves and, after we've cut your stinking man-hours and filled a great order for another customer, you hand us a $10 bonus.

We're sick and tired of your bullshit, Bob. And we're not going to take it. Not one second longer.

We haven't taken any disciplinary action against you, Bob, we've just stopped working. You may fear you're not going to keep getting rich by bleeding us and our lives dry, but that's not true. Your customers are waiting for you and their orders are still on the table.

But they're going to stay on the damned table until we get back a little of the wealth we create for you, Bob.

We're asking that you get a conscience, Bob. We are
requiring that you take a long look in the mirror and realize
what a drag it is for the rest of us to have to see you. We've
had to see you and put up with what you represent so damned
long that we're willing to risk our jobs to fix it, to make it
good. Discipline us all you want. Bring it on.

We all want JeffBoat to be a good place to work where
working people can make enough money to support our
families, to be sure we are safe and can return to them in
health, to be treated with some dignity and respect.

Thanks,

for absolutely nothing,

Metro United Up Yours Committee

People laughed at my response to Mr. Greene but several brought
up the fact that what I wrote could easily be taken as threatening.
"You said 'We haven't taken any disciplinary action against you,
Bob.' That's a clear threat," a fellow on the line at gate five told
me. I pointed out to him that I merely copied that line from Bob's
letter to us.

Interestingly, the letter from the president of the union
sounded very similar to Mr. Greene's letter. It was dated earlier
but arrived the same time as Bob's missive so it must have been
mailed late. That union just couldn't find good secretarial assistance. Regardless, my fellow workers and I were getting very
popular by not working, more popular than we had ever been by
doing our jobs well. His letter read:

April 30, 2001

Dear JeffBoat Employees:

We explained to JeffBoat employees this morning that Local 89
has not authorized a strike at JeffBoat.

The company has notified us that the Union's notice of re-
opening the contract was not sent to the Company 60 days

prior to contract expiration on April 29, 2001. Therefore, the contract automatically renews for an additional one year, until April 29, 2002. This includes the nostrike clause.

It is important that all JeffBoat employees end their strike and report to work. JeffBoat has the right to discipline, and perhaps discharge, employees for violating the no-strike clause. We do not want anyone to put his or her job in jeopardy. Therefore, we urge you to return to work.

We are doing our very best along with your negotiating committee, to find a way to solve this problem and get the best contract we can. We will report to you as soon as we have more information.

Fraternally,

Fred Zuckerman

President

I didn't want him to feel left out so I wrote him back, too.

May 3, 2001

Dear Fred Zuckerman:

We no longer give a damn what you did or did not explain to us.

The company may notify you about any contract it wants, but we workers have no contract. And so we have no "no-strike" clause.

We find it pretty damn disturbing that you – our representative – and the company are so friendly with one another. Maybe you don't see why that bothers us so let me tell you why: You see, we work hard. We weld. We drive cranes. We rig and fit steel and put in piping and paint and try and figure out the crappy blueprints the company gives us. With our brains and our hands we create the wealth that makes the world run – and that makes scum like you rich.

But even though it is we – the workers – who make the

world come alive through our labor, the wealth we create is pinched out of our hands and put into the pockets of stock-holders and company management. Isn't that a shame? The working person – the person that makes the wealth – is poor and the parasite who sits on their head is rich.

When you think about that, you realize that we working people have to stick together so that we can slowly make the world a good and fair place by putting wealth back into the hands of the people who made it, who deserve to reap the full fruit of their labor. We call that sort of sticking together, a "union."

Now Fred, when you betray working people and plot behind their backs, that's not a union. That's treachery and betrayal. You're a coward, Fred, and a scab. We urge you to take a flying fuck.

JeffBoat Workers' Flying Squadron for Truth and Justice

I printed my response to Mr. Zuckerman, too, and brought it with me. The point of responding to these letters was not to address anything said in them by Greene or Zuckerman. Nothing either said was of any interest to us. The point was to show that we could speak, too, and to highlight the arrogance and stupidity of their words. They thought they would belittle and scare us, but we were already belittled, every day, and we lived in fear of losing the tiny toehold of security we had in the world.

*

In the wee hours of that night, I was serenaded by Tom and Shitty Mike. Mike dug an old still out of a shed on his dad's acre in the woods and used it to bring a bit of relief to his friends on the picket line. It didn't hurt, his guitar playing. In between their playing they were trying to tell stories or jokes but these couldn't find semantic coherence in those lost hours and they ended up laughing loud and long, at nothing whatsoever. At some point in the moonlight concert, a banjo joined them and I saw it was Bob and beside him William slept in a chair.

"It's three am, Bob," I laughed, "isn't this past your bedtime?"

He smiled. "This is my last run. I'm retiring. Gonna do a bit of farming and spend time with my grandkids."

He picked on his banjo for a second, then looked at me again. "And play this thing, too."

"When do you retire?" I asked him.

"Now!" I'm supposed to be gone! But we had this to do and it's important so, um, right when we get back."

I felt like congratulating Bob on surviving the toxic weld smoke he had breathed for years, the dangerous conditions, the company's disregard for his life and limb, but the hidden anger in that thought was out of place with the music.

*

I walked along the street and spread my arms. In a real but alien sense, we were free for that time. This was an occupied zone, our occupied zone, and I couldn't stop laughing.

Angela was right that we were broke and that we lived paycheck-to-paycheck though one didn't cause the other. We were broke because we weren't paid enough. And our paycheck-to-paycheck condition began to hit home as day three of the wildcat arrived and no money was coming in. This would end our strike if it continued long enough as most of us had families, and even if we didn't we couldn't survive for long with no income. I began to ponder how this sort of thing, a strike, happened before, before any strikes were legal. Back then people pooled their money. They put their own strike funds together. They helped one another by sharing food or other work that might cost money. I read that in the case of several long and historically-important strikes, children would be sent off to live with friends and family members to ensure they were cared for properly, and to ensure their safety as well. We had little of this available to us and we were that much weaker for it.

Midday Thursday Mueller handed me a printout of an email exchange between someone in company administration and a couple of foremen. The administrator was concerned that the strike wasn't showing any sign of ending or weakening, and representatives for the Vane Brothers, the company that commissioned the ocean-going vessel work, were supposed to tour the shipyard. In fact, JeffBoat put up a billboard announcement about the ocean-going contract welcoming them and celebrating the agreement. JeffBoat's administrators wanted to show them an efficiently run yard and a docile workforce, and the wildcat strike smashed these plans. Any photo of the billboard would most likely include men and women with upraised middle fingers.

That apparently was too much for at least someone who sat behind a desk in the administration building and they informed several foremen of how to resolve the problem. Simply get two or three foremen to drive a white, company pickup truck over us. Do it fast and straight on. The administrator predicted that some of us would be armed and, when we saw our fellow workers crushed or killed, we'd certainly get violent. That would give the company an excuse to call the state police or even the National Guard, if the local police force refused to act.

I drove home late that afternoon to clean up and get something to eat. In my mail was a letter from the Teamsters which stated there would be a general meeting on Sunday morning, May 6, at 8 am. The International Vice President of the Teamsters, Walt Lytle, would be conducting the meeting. Later that night I spoke with other workers about what we thought might happen at the meeting and we all surmised that the Lytle would try and make good with us. We had demonstrated we were willing to go to extremes to defend our interests and the union showed their hand in working against us and for the company. We had circulated a petition to hold a decertification vote to get rid of the Teamsters. With all of this, what option was left to them but to try to get back in our good graces?

*

Thursday night some of the local activists distributed hot meals and sandwiches and other people – more random locals, supporters, family members – brought more ice chests and bins of food and drinks and folks along the picket line assisted in passing these around. My wife was there helping, too, and Rupe approached her asking for a sandwich and a bottle of water. She had never met him but recognized him from my paintings and drawings. When she handed him his food, she introduced herself and studied his face. His skull was large and his cheekbones were prominent in a very Germanic way. To me, in painting him, I was attracted to some contradictions I discovered in his face. The heavy skull and the kind features, the sense of alertness and intelligence in his eyes that I rendered most authentically by removing the light from them. He walked the picket line at night since he worked the second shift and those hours were familiar to him. I saw him under the glow of the street lights which accentuated the power of his face. My wife described a similar impression when she met him appearing out of the night like a rocky outcropping illuminated by a slash of lightning.

"Terry said you were beautiful."

She said he winced before he faded back into the darkness.

*

We settled into our routine by Friday and Saturday and the street and picket line became relatively calm. This was our street now. We slept there, cooked there, talked to one another there. No one tried to throw us off it and, at that point, it seemed no one could remove us. We had become a family. The news of the wildcat had spread and more deliveries came to us: truckloads of more water and pizzas, among other things. I recall an iconic scene, an emblem of the end of that week. A fellow had torn a sheet in half and tied it to the fencing around a parking lot. On this sheet he had written, "We're here for our children's future!" In front of this sheet, he placed a barbeque and a number of chairs. He brought stacks of paper plates and plastic utensils so that he could hand out food to anyone who needed it. I passed by him midday Saturday and, as I passed, I mentioned the meeting scheduled for Sunday morning.

"Hey, brother," he stated, kindly and defiantly, "I'll be here til it ends."

*

Sunday morning a group of union activists from the IWW lined the street in front of the union hall, some holding a banner that read, "An Injury to One is An Injury to All!" – the classic phrase from both the IWW and the Knights of Labor. Among them was a train conductor from Texas, a truck driver from Detroit, a preacher from Ohio, a crane operator from Indiana. The crane operator entered the union hall with me and we both felt the shaking air. The Teamsters' Vice President was on stage looking through some papers. An extremely muscular white man stood beside him wearing a short-sleeved knit shirt and sporting a salt-and-pepper mustache and goatee; he seemed like Sigmund Freud if Freud had preppy taste in clothing, a gym membership and no cancer of the jaw. I looked around, noticed that at least six, beefy Sigmund Freuds lined the union hall, each, like the man on the stage, with his hands together, his arms in front of him.

Walt took to the podium at the center front of the stage and spoke into the mic.

"Okay, people, let's get seated and get this thing moving. We have business to attend to."

There were over five-hundred of us and we all sat down nearly simultaneously.

Walt sighed and leaned into the mic.

"You're not going to like what I'm going to say, but that's how it's going to be, so listen up."

I already wanted to punch him in the face.

"Now the company put a great offer on the table and, as someone who's looking out for your interests, I'm telling you to vote it in."

"We already voted on the damn thing!" a number of us yelled back and Walt shook his head.

"You're not using your heads. That vote didn't count."

Mueller, along with a number of others, stood up and hollered at Walt that a second vote on a "final offer" was prohibited by National Labor Relations Board regulations as well as the Teamsters constitution. I felt the agitation spread across the room. Two Sigmunds carried a table to the foot of the stage and on that table sat a large, white, wooden box. Walt pointed to the box.

"We're gonna count ballots right here today and we're going to make sure you make the right decision."

The room was silent for a moment then two men leapt up and grabbed the box, turned it over and held it high to show that nothing was in it. Two Sigmunds walked toward the men.

"You fucking crook!" someone shouted. "No one trusts this union! You're in bed with the company!"

The men placed the box back on the table and took their seats.

"Ok, you people have gotten that out your system, now you're gonna vote and you're gonna approve this contract."

I felt the room squirm again. Walt stepped back from the microphone.

"Anybody's got a problem with this, let's hear it now."

I looked at Shaun who sat to my right. We were in the first row and I could see those who sat near me looked at one another nervously. Shaun and I locked eyes for a moment then Crowley, who sat on the other side of Shaun, noticed us.

"It's an invitation," I told Shaun.

He shook his head and his eyes glanced up and over at the handful of Sigmunds on the stage.

"Damn, man," he said and shook his head. "I got your back though."

Crowley heard him and his face registered shock for a moment, but he caught himself and whispered, "I'm gonna come flying up there to help, brother."

Whoever got onto that stage would have to turn his or her back to the Sigmunds and they'd descend on him. It seemed like a guaranteed beating. My stomach turned sour. I slapped Shaun's thigh and off I went.

Walt seemed shocked when I approached the stage. He looked straight ahead when he issued his challenge and didn't see me coming up his right flank, but there I was. He backed up as I took the podium. For a mere second, I was terrified to give my back to the Sigmunds; one against five or six are awful odds, especially when you're pointed in the wrong direction. I adjusted the mic and looked up to see hundreds of unsure people who sat nervously on metal chairs. Five-hundred to six were odds I could accept.

"This is bullshit!" I spoke into the mic and folks clapped. I could feel the Sigmunds behind me. I pulled the mic off its stand and walked to the front of the stage.

"We voted on a contract and we rejected the contract. The reasons we rejected the contract haven't changed. What's changed is that someone's trying to force us to accept the damned thing now!" People clapped and whistled. "To hell with this!" I yelled. "Let's get out of these chairs!" and the crowd rose. I walked off the stage and onto the floor. "We need to get rid of this union. We struck without them and we've been successful. They have nothing to offer except a knife in the back!"

Mueller came running up to me and I handed him the mic. He yelled about the Rank-and-File Slate and voting out the union officials and the rigged election. He yelled about filing more grievances. Paul tapped on his arm and Mueller handed him the mic.

"This is all bullshit, people."

Paul held the mic for a few more seconds, long enough for the crowd to quiet up a bit.

"Fuck the world!" he stated and everyone cheered.

More and more people approached the stage, took the mic, and aired their beef. Finally, Lytle asked if we could move on to voting and several guys in the back of the hall picked up chairs and threw them against the wall. "Fuck you, dude!" one roared.

Walt directed us to the voting booths in the right of the union hall. We formed two long lines and the Sigmunds walked down the lines, brushed against us, whispered to each person, "This is a good contract. Vote it in. Don't mess around."

Someone ahead of me in line raised his hand and shouted, "Got a no vote here!" and he looked at the closest Sigmund.

"A no vote here, too!" someone else joined in and it became a chorus. I raised my ballot, too, and shouted my no vote into the crowd. Walt stood on stage with his hands on his hips and glared at us.

Two men counted the ballots in front of Walt while we waited. The vote was five-hundred against the contract, twenty-three in favor, and one vote of "Fuck you!" Walt announced the results and dropped his head in disgust when he read the last, single vote which, as we all knew, was directed at him. He slowly walked to the podium.

"Ok, then. You're working under the same lousy contract you have been working under for another year while this gets worked out."

"You assholes negotiated that contract, too!" someone yelled at him and a wave of ferocious laughter pealed through the auditorium.

After the vote some of us gathered for a meeting at a local activist center. We discussed what might lie ahead for us and what the company and the union might try to do to us. We had all been focused on what was going on immediately in front of us and, as we talked about the past week, it was beginning to occur to us that we had lived through a great event. Looking around me I realized we had new faces.

*

On Thursday, May 10, I received a letter from the union. I dreaded opening the letter since nothing good ever came from either the union or the company, two evil giants who clearly shared interests with one another and none with me. This letter was a notice of a meeting. On Sunday, May 19, 2001, at 8 am, the union would hold a general meeting at the Ramada Inn. This was strange since the union owned a hall with an ample auditorium. And of course, once again, the meeting was held on a day and at an hour intended to limit the number of workers attending.

I arrived at the Ramada Inn and the first thing I noticed was the greatly increased security surrounded the relatively small hotel. Police cars, private security cars, a state police car. Must be a very uplifting meeting the Teamsters planned for us.

The meeting room at Ramada was packed: maybe there were three-hundred of us there. No one appeared to keep an official count that day. In fact nothing seemed official or certain especially since we were not supposed to be voting a second time on a strike vote, on a final offer, and yet here we were voting for a third time, and this time with double or maybe triple the security of the previous meeting. The business agent and the president of the local sat at a long, folding table at the front of the room and on the center of the table was placed a podium and a microphone.

Walt Lytle was back again, and he informed us that we would be voting again today. Shouting began, but our eyes focused on the many officers in the room, all armed, ready to haul us off. Walt told us the contract was good and we were going to vote it in, then he turned over the microphone to Zuckerman and he repeated what Lytle said. They asked if we had any questions and we did, along with other words, too, but every time we rose to speak, the security men tensed and prepared to advance. We were on lockdown, yet we still spoke against this third vote, against what had happened, the safety violations, the harassment, the lies.

A woman rose to speak and, notably, security did not react to her. She was a white lady with frizzy brown hair, and she wore a short-sleeved, white t-shirt with two packs of cigarettes rolled upward in the sleeves of each arm. Her words were angry but her voice was low and Lytle asked if she could speak louder, but instead she left her seat and stepped into the aisle between the rows of metal chairs, the open aisle that led to the table with the podium, that led to Lytle and Zuckerman. She spoke again and began walking forward and we realized she was calling them names, cursing them, threatening them, her arms out to her sides as though she were going to attack. Security understood the situation about the same time as the rest of us, when this woman was about six feet from the table, but they stood on the perimeter of the crowd and, if this woman chose to leap onto our local's president or Lytle, nothing could be done. We began to cheer her with barred teeth as she walked closer and closer, cursing and snarling. "Fuck 'em up!" someone yelled and we all began to shout similar suggestions. A couple of feet before the table, she stopped, pointed her finger in their faces, yelled and threatened, then turned and walked back to her seat.

The room hovered on a ledge, ready to tumble over it into uncontrollable fury. As our shouting began to dim, Lytle asked for a show of hands over the contract and no one voted for it. Lytle started making additional sounds with his mouth but we left, silently, got into our cars and trucks and went home.

*

Monday at lunch I headed close to the river's edge to be alone and to draw. On my way I saw William who stood outside of the breakroom and seemed to stare at the side of the building. He said nothing as I passed which was very unusual for him. I put my hand on his shoulder and asked if he was alright.

"No, I'm not," he confessed and continued to stare at the wall. "Bob had a heart attack."

I walked around to face him. "When did you find out?"

"This morning." He wept. "Bob was my buddy."

I stayed two hours past the end of shift for overtime. As I walked toward gate eight to go home, the late spring sun seemed to wash all the details from around me, leaving me with soft areas of low-angled color like a stream shielded by thick trees. One of the operators of a gantry crane crossed my path. He was a second-shift worker and I didn't know his name but he was on the picket line with me at gate five during the wildcat. I remembered him as the man who jumped across Angela's pickup truck after she tried to plow into us.

"Hey, buddy," he shouted and walked over to me, "we won!"

I smiled and he grabbed my hand and shook it, but before I could consider what to say, I had both my hands on his, shaking enthusiastically.

"I guess we did," I told him, then we laughed, "I guess we actually did."

He strolled back to his job and, when he was about thirty or so feet away, he turned and hollered, "That was one of the greatest moments of my life, my friend!"

I headed toward the gate. From behind me a woman shouted,

"Hey!" and I turned to see her. She lit a cigarette and the gray smoke swirled around her grime-and sweatlaced face.

"Yeah, dude" she said, "we won. What are we gonna do now?"

Epilogue: Reflections from Over a Decade Away

I chose to end the story of the JeffBoat wildcat strike at this point but the tale continues. However, some of the events that followed in the months after the end of the wildcat, events that directly impacted what transpired in the shipyard, extend far beyond the scope of this book. The effect of those events, along with the use of that effect nationally by those in power at the time, warrants its own telling independent of the strike. The strike ended May 6, 2001 and the events I'm referring to are the attacks of September 11, 2001.

The period of time following the wildcat was an amazing one. There was no workplace animosity coming from the company, no attempts to get us to jeopardize our lives for our jobs, no gratuitous firings or suspensions. It was clear, or seemed to be clear to most of us, that the company and the union intended to leave us alone in order to avoid further trouble for further trouble was exactly what we were prepared to cause them if we were provoked. But independent of the absence of harassment by the company and the union, and the peace that arose from that absence, something happened to us because of our actions in creating and maintaining the wildcat strike, an illegal strike that was strong, supportive and free of violence against one another. The thing that happened is we changed. We began to look after one another. The daily anger disappeared and we approached each other with friendliness. We checked on each other's lives, asked questions about how things were going, took concern for the welfare of the people around us. To give a small but specific example: every morning after the so-called safety meeting, an argument or harsh exchange would break out as we competed over weld lines. But the morning after the strike, and almost every morning thereafter, we hooked up lines for other people and there were few if any arguments about this.

This outbreak of compassion, of goodness (though that word has been conjoined with weakness and naiveté in contemporary American culture), is something that appears to happen to many people in the wake of a catastrophe. I've seen this take place after Hurricane Sandy here in New York as well as in the case of the many floods and tornadoes I witnessed growing up in Kentucky and during the long time I lived there as an adult. This goodness presents itself, to me at least, as a feeling – and it is definitely accompanied by cluster of emotions – but I believe it's something more exotic and yet fundamental, something I picture as new soil to walk on or a return to an unknown, familiar and welcoming home. This sort of experience awakens something in us and the thing that wakes up pours out into society at large.

The JeffBoat Wildcat Strike of 2001 did just that. Its achievement inspired a number of actions regionally, nationally and internationally; most of these went underreported or even unreported in the media, though a number appeared in the alternative (at that time) venue of the Internet. I was in control of the main email address related to the wildcat and I received many emails from people who had heard of what we did and felt stronger about making positive change in their workplaces. There was a great joy among those people who contacted me as there was among us at the shipyard, a joy that comes from having a say about your life and how you choose to live it.

Here's an example of a bit of that spirit from later in 2001, from the fall of that year, an example that unfortunately ties us to the next phase of the situation at JeffBoat. The workers at Plumbers Supply on Market Street in Louisville went on strike on the first of September, 2001. Their complaints were the usual of low pay, high insurance rates, unfair company policies and so forth. When they went on strike, the company threatened to fire them, hire replacements and break their union, the Teamsters (though not Local 89, the local that misrepresented us at

JeffBoat). I began contacting people in the area, asking them if we could form what we whimsically referred to as a "Flying Squadron." This was a group of people who agreed to sit in on a picket line, bring food and drinks, and in general be supportive, just like the sort of support we had received at JeffBoat. On September 10, 2001, I made a series of calls to supporters and good people across the Louisville area to see who wanted to show up the next day and other days that week. Quite a few people were interested and willing. That second week of September, 2001, would have been a massive show of strength and we had the numbers and energy at that point.

The morning of September 11, 2001, I was working in the pipe shop at JeffBoat when the shop phone rang. The call was for me and I thought it was another person committing to join the picket line at Plumbers Supply. Instead it was a friend of mine telling me that the US was under attack. New York City was under attack. The World Trade Center had been bombed. After that call, I received no return calls from people going to help the folks at Plumbers Supply ever again. All attention turned to the Wahhabists from Saudi Arabia who attacked the World Trade Center and the Pentagon, and then to Bush and his war on Afghanistan and Iraq (and away from his administration's looting of the economy of the United States).

About a month after the attacks the company began a series of meetings with us. These were small meetings with no more than twenty or so of us gathered at a time. The company had administrators or some group they hired to bring in a collection of charts and big pads of paper and place these on an easel. While pointing at the graphs and little pictures on these items, these folks explained to us that there was a structure to American business. There was the company, the stockholders and the workers. In one of these lessons, the triangle replaced the company with the government. They explained that the company was doing great financially and had to share this profit with the stockholders (or, in the one instance, generously give some to the government) but couldn't share that prosperity with us. The fact the company and stockholders couldn't share profit with us was explained to us very unclearly by these charts and pictures, but the upshot was that our contract couldn't give us a raise or take care of our insurance. If we understood that we couldn't get anything for our work, we would understand that another wildcat next year was pointless. The company, the stockholders and even the government could return nothing. To strike at all, to harm American business, was a form of terrorism since it wounded America. In fact, to cause problems on the job at all was aiding America's enemies.

A few of us were stupid enough to buy this lie, but most didn't. And we saw the sweat coming off the foreheads of the liars sent to swindle us. But we didn't know what to do about it. I'll relate an incident to show the temper of that time, the fear the company and union displayed toward us. I arrived at one of these meetings late and I came in the wrong door, an entrance that put me behind the charts and behind a union steward and the chief steward, Tiny, who stood in the shadows and backed this line of crap we were being fed. I stood there, behind them, and when I realized they were nervous, I didn't remove my hardhat or goggles but remained in formation so to speak, glaring, black screens for eyes. The union steward backed up and whispered to me, asking me if I would like to have a seat, and I said nothing. Later that day I was told by a fellow worker that this union steward was worried about me and my underground army. This was of course patently ridiculous as no one was underground but in fact sitting in chairs and at tables in front of everyone and there was no army, just a lot of people trying to do their jobs and live their lives and finding that task impossible given the doublefisted obstacle of the company and the union.

At the conclusion of the meetings, they passed out tiny American-flag stickers, which we were supposed to put on our hardhats. We had won, at least in the substantial sense of staying strong against overwhelming odds, but we felt defeated. The company was against us, the union was against us, the government was against us, the president was against us, the terrorists were against us. And of course wherever we looked, on every screen at least was the snarling face of Dick Cheney, a horrible jack-o'-lantern streaking through the consciousness screens of the nation.

Between that fall and the next spring, many people left the shipyard, looking for work in other places in the area. None of us wanted to be there in the first place but we were trapped by necessity, and when everything – low pay, safety violations, lousy insurance – is equal except for a demoralized workplace, why not move on? Many of the strongest people we had there were gone, along with our determination.

When the contract came up for renewal, we struck and the union supported us, gave us strike pay, and negotiated a deal that was barely better than the contract we struck over in the wildcat a year before. If those events of September had not happened, things would almost certainly have gone very differently. I hate to relate these things since it seems like a confession of weakness, but ultimately we, like most of the participants in history, fell for a con, the con of history.

There was a decertification vote at JeffBoat in 2006 and there have been a number of deaths since then. I want to mention some of these to you. In May of 2010, two people lost their lives at JeffBoat. One of these was Robert Harrison, Jr. He had worked at JeffBoat for eighteen years and he fell from a ladder to his death in the cargo hull of a barge. I've worked with these out-of-date, rickety ladders and I'm surprised more people are not dead from them. A week later, David Martin fell and died. He was forty-four years old. At the point of Martin's death, OSHA reported thirty-eight serious safety violations at JeffBoat since 1985. Then in 2011, Steven Duncan was crushed between "equipment" (I have no idea what this means as there is a lot of equipment around) and a barge. He was fifty-four years old. Again, in 2015, Sergio Torrente, age forty, died of so-called "mysterious" causes while working in the keel of a barge around nine am.

I'm writing this in 2015 and the same folks are in power in the company and in the union (as well as, I feel confident asserting, the parent company, and the corporate umbrella, CitiCorp). And despite the wildcat strike and all of the attention it garnered, despite the 2006 attempt at decertification, and the deaths of more and more workers, and the tremendous effort these workers, including myself, have thrown against this congregation of evil, very little has changed.

What does it mean that little has changed? What insights can we draw from this lack of progress? How are we to conceive of a world in which so much energy and blood is devoted to barely loosening a thread in the fabric of power?

One key element in this conundrum is our memory. I think it's paramount to note that we do not remember a certain enormous set of events. Though there was global support within labor and activist communities for what was occurring at JeffBoat and I am sure that many of those people clearly remember that time, those who worked there afterward almost certainly heard little about what had taken place. In part this is because it is not in the company's or the union's interests that people under their power recall these events. That observation can be expanded to reflect the global monoculture of power as well.

It is of little consequence that we remember the streams, the flora and the fauna of an area that is now a subdivision, but it is of great consequence that we remember the titles on that land held by families and the acquisition of these titles by developers and corporate interests, and it is of further interest to note subsequent corporate or wealthy individual owners. It is vital to know how much money these title-holders have made from the land and how much more there is to be made. Similarly, if you read the history of JeffBoat (or almost any other large company) or if you visit the museum across the street from JeffBoat, you encounter a concentration of memories telling the story of JeffBoat's owners, the story of how the things made at JeffBoat were utilized by other companies or by the US government, the achievements of JeffBoat's administration and its parent company. The people who worked there, whose creations are the very reason for JeffBoat's existence, are noted and there are photos of some of them along with their tools, but these images are displayed more as curiosities or, at best, as secondary incidents, the relatively insignificant details of the implementation of the desires of power (company, government, corporate entity). The workers – or "workforce" – are unnamed and of course their lives, their injuries, and their deaths are unmentioned.

What we do remember is a set of emotions and representations that are directed and managed, and those memories to which we are directed are sanctioned memories. Memories of workplace, of ecosystem, of community, are unsanctioned. They are not considered worthy of being transmitted through time and so they do not cohere into the larger pattern that forms our understanding of the world and what we take to be the "meaning" of human life. And it is from our understanding of the world and its meaning that our actions arise. If our conception of the world only involves a set of sanctioned memories, memories whose importance is not questioned – ownership, transfer of ownership, money, significance in terms of war or for us by those in power for control or further acquisition – that conception of the structure of the world legitimizes elite control and abuse while simultaneously rendering unimportant, invalid, or inconsequential other stories. And as long as we conceive of the world through the prism of sanctioned memories – the majority of which are not only against our interests but are also false – our actions will most likely have little or no lasting effect.

Note what is missing from sanctioned memory for that

missing component is not simply the grand events, the heroic-sounding moments, but the at least equally important, day-to-day tasks we undertake to cope with the demands put on us by the needs of those in power. I'm referring to activities like preparing the meals we take to work, getting from our homes to work, repairing our bodies from the damage done to them in the normal work routine (not to mention the illegal and unwritten demands of a company like JeffBoat regarding safety – or, for that matter, many of the other companies for which I have worked), maintaining our relationships in spite of extreme mental and physical stress, our interests and pursuits outside of work, and our efforts to hold back the more straightforwardly life-threatening demands of power. All of these actions factor into the history of JeffBoat as a workplace, as a site, but they do not constitute its history or ours and so are "unsanctioned" memories.

We take it for granted that many of these actions – preparing lunch or so-called "outside interests" – should not be included as part of a workplace history, but why do we take it for granted? Why is it an obvious point that money, ownership and the role played in the maintenance of power are the central facts of a workplace? For that to be an obvious point, a decision or set of decisions had to be made about what is valuable, a decision that is now forgotten, and it is in part this subterranean decision and our consent to its dictates that denudes us of our effectiveness. If we knew of these unsanctioned memories, recounted them and valued them as part of our history and part of the history of a place or institution, we could build on our efforts and accomplishments. Doing this, however, would ultimately render us uncontrollable to those in power, for it is on this directed forgetting that much of power rests.

Further hindering our potential to change the universe is the strangulation of our ability to dream, to imagine. Many people, at least within the United States, appear unable to conceive of a way of living different from the way they are living now. Likewise those of us involved in the wildcat strike at JeffBoat could not imagine much beyond striking and getting better pay and better insurance, and so forth, if we succeeded. There have been many ways we humans have organized ourselves. Some of these ways led to more freedom and some did not, some allowed for great achievements and some did not, but our contemporary social order is integrated with a political and technological system that seems to rule out all options whatsoever. If we were to radically change things how could we power our refrigerators and computers? To do so means using electricity which means doing business with a utility company. How can we obtain such necessities as food, clothing or an education without extending our hands through the one window available to us?

We are currently almost incapable of understanding the options available to us and one principal culprit of rendering us helpless in this sense, of reducing our capacity for imaginative diversity, is education. At one time the purpose of education was the expansion of our possibilities, the achievement of a greater ability to conceive and conceptualize, and greater creative power. Education today is not only often a form of vocational training, it is a purposeful indoctrination in powerlessness and short-sightedness, a denuding of vision. What happened after the wildcat was in some respect a result of our inability to imagine something else as well as political utilization of the terrorist attacks.

What is that "something else" we fail to imagine? In a straightforward sense, "something else" is a collection of possibilities, an assembly of "What If"s, all of them revolving around the ways we might organize ourselves as a society, the manner in which we could live our lives together and individually. But beyond this immediate sense of "something else," this group of various, concrete options, I feel there is another way to understand the thing we can no longer imagine, this unsanctioned shadow dream. We can picture this other meaning of "something else" as not merely any set of particular options or possibilities, but rather as the raw possibility of things being otherwise.

This raw possibility is the opposite of the managed, global monoculture we live in at present; the former is an unfolding of ever-evolving potential and the latter, a forced lack of choice, a selection of one. I suggest we picture the relation between this raw possibility, this very ground of the possible, and our homogenous, monitored culture not as a relation between what doesn't exist and what does exist but rather as the relation between what could exist and what does in fact exist. This sort of relation was introduced by certain German thinkers in the eighteenth and nineteenth centuries (and, if it wasn't, it's of no concern to me in this book) as the relation between insistence and existence. Insistence is the quality possessed by those things that could be, but are not, by what we can no longer imagine. Insistence is the potential for things to be otherwise.

This notion of the quality of insistence may appear to carry with it the implication that the raw possibility that things could be otherwise is itself related to the demand that things should be otherwise. On that understanding, the raw possibility that things could be otherwise would simply be a form of the idea of progress. But I see the raw possibility that things could be otherwise as the result of human imagination and our ability to fantasize, not as the unfolding of an innate moral, social or political essence or even the nature of scientific inquiry and development. On that portrayal, progress in the moral, social, political, scientific and even spiritual sense is not inevitable but still attainable and can be presented as a choice for which we can argue. But for there to be the possibility of choices outside the allowance of our monoculture, we must be able to conceive of these alternatives, and that we cannot presently do.

In addition to control of our memories and imagination, there is the problem of work itself or, more accurately stated, of "unwork." Most of the tasks that occupy our daily lives bear little relation to anything we consider important. Those tasks function to distract us from consideration of our alternatives in conception or action. It's my suspicion that at least some of the tension we experience in our contemporary work environments is not merely the result of poor working conditions or meaningless toil, but the product of repressing the raw possibility of doing something else, something potentially meaningful. Along with this horrible feeling of wasting our lives and not being able to see a way out of that trap, our contemporary workplaces are littered with surveillance equipment that, I claim, is not simply there to make sure we do our assigned tasks – which it is in a direct and local sense – but, viewed against the backdrop of unwork, is there to make sure we do nothing else. For if we did explore our options, we might discover that most of what we do as "work" is totally unnecessary, is an obstacle to living a rewarding, human life, and is perhaps even toxic to life on Earth.

I began this book looking for the answer to my impression that the world was a prison. The Prison is the thing that prevents human society from happening; that substitutes a managed, prescribed existence for the possibilities of human creativity. What makes the world a prison is our unawareness of this state of things.

A Song Written About the JeffBoat Wildcat Strike

Wildcat on the Ohio

Well, there's a group of workers on the Ohio,
They got their jobs without a resume or bio,
They build the barges and the ships that sail far and wide'o,
Little did they know their trade union was a lie'o.

So all you kittens, all you cats, salty dogs and river rats,
We're shutting down this stinkin' job tomorrow,
We've had enough, we call your bluff, this Wildcat is hanging
    tough,
On Big Grand Union on the OhHiOh.

JeffBoat works them in the pouring rain and lightning all the
    time'o,
Boss sends them down to burnin' holds just to make a dime'o,
A socalled contract wasn't signed, it never saw their eye'o,
The workers said we've had enough, let's hit the picket line'o.

So all you kittens, all you cats, salty dogs and river rats,
We're shutting down this stinkin' job tomorrow,
We've had enough, we call your bluff, this Wildcat is hanging
    tough,
On Big Grand Union on the OhHiOh.

All you workers in this land, come together, lend a hand,
JeffBoat workers cannot do it solo,
Send your food, and send some cash, let's kick both bosses in
    the ass,
This Wildcat will strike on the Ohio.

So all you kittens, all you cats, salty dogs and river rats,
We're shutting down this stinkin' job tomorrow,
We've had enough, we call your bluff, this Wildcat is hanging
    tough,
On Big Grand Union on the OhHiOh.

*Composed Saturday, June 2, 2001 by the UpMidPOC Peck Farm
Songwriters Collective.*

Glossary of Some Workplace Terms Used

Gunnel (or sometimes called the "Gunwale"): the top of the side of a boat or the topmost plank of a wooden vessel.

Kevel: a kevel is a simple thing, easier drawn than described. A dictionary definition is "a sturdy cleat for securing a line, as in mooring a ship." It looks like a rounded set of steer horns if a steer were somewhat runty and made of metal.

Wildcat strike: a strike action undertaken by unionized workers without union authorization, support or approval; this is sometimes referred to as an unofficial industrial action; an illegal strike.

Slate: a list of candidates for election to a post or office, usually gathered together as a group sharing a set of political views.

Rake/bow: the front of ship or boat. In the case of barges, the front is usually referred to as the "rake."

Stern: the back of a boat or ship.

Starboard: the right side of a ship or boat if your anus is pointed at the stern.

Portside: the left side of a ship or boat if your anus is pointed at the stern.

Arc-welding: a technique in which metals are welded using heat generated by an electric arc.

Stinger: the electrode holder for an arc-welding machine.

Rod: the stick of flux-coated metal you place in the stinger for arc-welding.

Coaming: the coaming is standardly defined as "a raised frame (as around a hatchway in the deck of a ship) to keep out water," but in open-ended/hopper barges, the coaming also keeps contents contained as in the case of grains or coal. It's sheet steel with a lip on it.

Zero Books
CULTURE, SOCIETY & POLITICS

Contemporary culture has eliminated the concept and public figure of the intellectual. A cretinous anti-intellectualism presides, cheer-led by hacks in the pay of multinational corporations who reassure their bored readers that there is no need to rouse themselves from their stupor. Zer0 Books knows that another kind of discourse - intellectual without being academic, popular without being populist - is not only possible: it is already flourishing. Zer0 is convinced that in the unthinking, blandly consensual culture in which we live, critical and engaged theoretical reflection is more important than ever before.

If you have enjoyed this book, why not tell other readers by posting a review on your preferred book site. Recent bestsellers from Zero Books are:

In the Dust of This Planet
Horror of Philosophy vol. 1
Eugene Thacker
In the first of a series of three books on the Horror of Philosophy, *In the Dust of This Planet* offers the genre of horror as a way of thinking about the unthinkable.
Paperback: 978-1-84694-676-9 ebook: 978-1-78099-010-1

Capitalist Realism
Is there no alternative?
Mark Fisher
An analysis of the ways in which capitalism has presented itself as the only realistic political-economic system.
Paperback: 978-1-84694-317-1 ebook: 978-1-78099-734-6

Rebel Rebel
Chris O'Leary
David Bowie: every single song. Everything you want to know, everything you didn't know.
Paperback: 978-1-78099-244-0 ebook: 978-1-78099-713-1

Cartographies of the Absolute
Alberto Toscano, Jeff Kinkle
An aesthetics of the economy for the twenty-first century.
Paperback: 978-1-78099-275-4 ebook: 978-1-78279-973-3

Malign Velocities
Accelerationism and Capitalism
Benjamin Noys
Long listed for the Bread and Roses Prize 2015, *Malign Velocities* argues against the need for speed, tracking acceleration as the symptom of the on-going crises of capitalism.
Paperback: 978-1-78279-300-7 ebook: 978-1-78279-299-4

Meat Market
Female flesh under Capitalism
Laurie Penny
A feminist dissection of women's bodies as the fleshy fulcrum of capitalist cannibalism, whereby women are both consumers and consumed.
Paperback: 978-1-84694-521-2 ebook: 978-1-84694-782-7

Poor but Sexy
Culture Clashes in Europe East and West
Agata Pyzik
How the East stayed East and the West stayed West.
Paperback: 978-1-78099-394-2 ebook: 978-1-78099-395-9

Romeo and Juliet in Palestine
Teaching Under Occupation
Tom Sperlinger
Life in the West Bank, the nature of pedagogy and the role of a
university under occupation.
Paperback: 978-1-78279-637-4 ebook: 978-1-78279-636-7

Sweetening the Pill
or How we Got Hooked on Hormonal Birth Control
Holly Grigg-Spall
Has contraception liberated or oppressed women? *Sweetening
the Pill* breaks the silence on the dark side of hormonal
contraception.
Paperback: 978-1-78099-607-3 ebook: 978-1-78099-608-0

Why Are We The Good Guys?
Reclaiming your Mind from the Delusions of Propaganda
David Cromwell
A provocative challenge to the standard ideology that Western
power is a benevolent force in the world.
Paperback: 978-1-78099-365-2 ebook: 978-1-78099-366-9

Readers of ebooks can buy or view any of these bestsellers by
clicking on the live link in the title. Most titles are published in
paperback and as an ebook. Paperbacks are available in traditional
bookshops. Both print and ebook formats are available online.

Find more titles and sign up to our readers' newsletter at
http://www.johnhuntpublishing.com/culture-and-politics
Follow us on Facebook at https://www.facebook.com/ZeroBooks
and Twitter at https://twitter.com/Zer0Books